America's Cup

Trials & Triumphs

"ANOTHER REACH, AND DON'T YOU WISH YOU MAY GET IT?"—From the *World* (New York).

1899

Uncle Sam teases John Bull with the Cup: "Another reach, and don't you wish you may get it?" New York World, *1899.*

America's Cup

Trials & Triumphs

Richard V. Simpson

Charleston · London

THE
History
PRESS

Published by The History Press
Charleston, SC 29403
www.historypress.net

Front cover images: Top Center: An image of the celebrated cup as it appeared in 1905
Top Left: Herreshoff's Defender, page 85.
Top Right: British challenger the Sceptre, page 142.
Bottom: The New York Yacht Club's 1888 Newport redezvous, page 27.

First published 2010

Manufactured in the United States

ISBN 978.1.59629.329.8

Library of Congress Cataloging-in-Publication Data

Simpson, Richard V.
The America's Cup : trials and triumphs / Richard V. Simpson.
p. cm.
Includes bibliographical references.
ISBN 978-1-59629-329-8
1. America's Cup--History. 2. Yacht racing--History. 3. Yachts--Design and construction--
History. I. Title.
GV829.S56 2010
797.1'4--dc22
2010014132

Contents

Foreword

The Race for the America's Cup

Over the seas now for the twelfth time [1903], *there has come a vessel in quest of the America's Cup. While the first of the races for the cup will not be sailed on the Sandy Hook course until August twentieth, increasing interest has been shown for weeks past. The fact that three fast yachts are striving for the honor of defending the trophy has given stimulus to the interest this year. Sir Thomas Lipton, the central figure in all this yachting enthusiasm, has come besieging this year with a small navy—the* Shamrocks, I *and* II, *each with a crew of over forty, the* [steam] *yacht* Erin, *manned by over half a hundred men, the sea-going tug* Cruizer, *and two American built launches. He has doggedly made this third expedition with his hundred and sixty seamen for a silver cup, twenty-seven inches high, which cost a hundred pounds. On this side of the Atlantic the preparations for defense has been quite as extensive. The challenge and defense of the Cup, first and last, will cost in the neighborhood of a million dollars.*

This international excitement is in peculiar contrast to the interest shown fifty-two years ago, when the America *defeated the flotilla of John Bull's fastest boats, and triumphantly brought the Cup back with it. Then, although the Yankee pilot-boat had won the first international yacht race with such apparent ease that there was "no second," there were practically no press notices of the event in this country and the reception that greeted the schooner on its arrival was only mildly enthusiastic. It was eighteen years before any challenger for the Cup crossed the Atlantic. In 1870 Mr. James Ashbury's* Cambria *sailed against an American flotilla of seventeen boats and was defeated by the* Dauntless. *Another Ashbury cutter, the* Livonia,* met defeat the following year, the Columbia and Sappho *each out sailing her twice. Mr. Ashbury had very justly protested against the unfairness of having to sail against a whole flotilla. After much spirited correspondence he carried his point for the races of 1871, when he sailed against only one of our yachts at a time.*

The Canadian challengers of 1876, and 1881 proved "easy" for the defenders. Then, in 1885 and 1886, came the Genesta *and* Galatea, *which were in turn vanquished by the Boston sloops* Mayflower *and* Puritan. *The coming of the Scotch cutter* Thistle *in 1887, which was defeated by the* Volunteer, *was a much more important event than any one supposed at the time. It was then that Sir Thomas Lipton decided that his country, too, at some time, should have a yacht challenger. The history of the* Valkyrie *races of 1893 and 1895, and of the defeats of the two* Shamrocks, *everybody still remembers.*

Years back, both challengers and defenders used to follow national lines pretty closely. The British boats were cutters, deep and narrow, with keels— craft especially suited to the deep, stormy, choppy British seas. The American vessels, on the other hand, were broad, shallow, center-board sloops, well adapted to our coast waters. From the time of the Puritan, *however, there has been a constant game of give-and-take, of borrowing right and left, until today, to the unsophisticated, at least,* Shamrock III *and* Reliance *look a good deal alike. The* Puritan *was built somewhat on the lines of the British cutter. In 1887 the* Volunteer *showed British traits; while the* Thistle, *built for the specific purpose of speed in American waters, copied the broad American beam, and has been called the first British racing machine. In 1895 the center-board became a back number—it was hard, too, to give up such a hobby—and Herreshoff built the* Defender *with an orthodox John Bull keel. Both the* Defender *and* Valkyrie *were out-and-out racing machines, cut away below the water-line, and carrying large areas of sail, the American boat being a cutter in everything but the name.*

International yacht racing of today unquestionably affords magnificent sport, and it has called forth remarkable ingenuity on the part of designers. Nevertheless, the present tendency in the construction of the ninety-footer is deplorable. The America, *built fifty-two years ago, was one of those pilot-boats of which for speed and usefulness, the American seaman was justly proud. It cost something like thirty thousand dollars, and is a staunch, serviceable craft today. The* Reliance, *good authority has it, cost over three hundred thousand dollars, and will be good for nothing but old junk. As one New York paper put it, Herreshoff's latest monstrosity is "a spar-*

deck between a bulb of lead and an acre of sail." When in 1870, the Cambria *came to this country as the first Cup challenger she raced James Gordon Bennett's* Dauntless *all the way across the Atlantic. The racer of today is such a delicate creature that it is really a great risk to let her get her feet wet.*

What the next turn of the screw in the development of ocean racing machines will lead to is an open question. It is to be hoped that common sense will once more come to the front and that real boats will again be pressed into service.

—*Oliver Bronson Copen, "The Race for the America's Cup,"* Country Life in America, *no. 4 (August 1903)*

Author's Note

The prehistory of American yachting and 150-plus-year history of the America's Cup, the oldest and most distinguished prize in the world of sport, is summarized in this book. The sport of ocean sailboat racing was and is generally the sport of wealthy barons of industry who can afford the titanic expenses involved in designing, building and rigging a large yacht—a pleasure that the average middle-class day sailor can only aspire to.

As a native Rhode Islander who has always lived within walking distance to Narragansett Bay, my experience on the briny has been limited to an occasional outboard motor-driven bass boat fishing for scup, flounder and blues. Regardless of my limited "sailing" experience, I was and continue to be exposed to, and admire, the majestic beauty of large sailing craft.

During my daily commute to my job in Newport during the early 1960s, I became keenly aware of the struggle for the honor of defending the America's Cup by competing 12-metre yachts in the race for the Goelet Cup, the winner of which would be pronounced Cup Defender.

It was a eureka! moment for me when I learned that so much of the significant history of America's Cup defenders is founded in my hometown of Bristol. It was then that I began collecting America's Cup–related ephemera; many of the words and pictures in this book are from my forty-year accumulation.

Generally, long sequences of directly quoted text are in the public domain; the source of this material is identified when known. All illustrations are from my collection; their sources, when known, are noted at the end of each illustration's caption.

This book is not meant as a definitive history of the event but rather an overview of some of the most interesting facts and figures of large sail, seagoing yacht racing for the land-bound sailor—in effect, a primer.

Acknowledgements

M y sincere appreciation goes to Halsey C. Herreshoff for allowing use of his first-person narrative *History of America's Cup Racing*. As grandson of Captain Nat Herreshoff, son of celebrated marine architect A. Sidney DeWolf Herreshoff and an active participant in twenty-five years of America's Cup races, his insights on twentieth-century Cup races add reliable authority and scholarship to this book.

Introduction

The America's Cup is a gaudy high Victorian ewer. It is the most cherished yachting trophy in existence. It is also the least beautiful to contemporary eyes, and as a ewer, it is useless because it has no bottom. It is silver-plated Britannia, an inexpensive base metal consisting of a composition of tin, antimony and copper. It is alleged that as many as six cups like this were crafted in 1848 by R&S Gerrard of England as off-the-shelf trophies. Sir Henry Paget, the Marques of Anglesey, purchased one and donated it as the prize for the Royal Yacht Squadron's 1851 annual regatta around the Isle of Wight.

The Cup was originally known by the Squadron as the "Royal Yacht Squadron Cup" or the "RYS Cup for One Hundred Sovereigns." Subsequently, the Cup became known, by the Americans who won it, as the Hundred-Guinea Cup because it cost 100 guineas to make, including labor. Today, as scrap metal, it would barely fetch $100. The Cup's price, however, has nothing to do with its value.

Britain's Prince Albert organized the first Industrial World's Fair, also known for a short period as Prince Albert's Great Exhibition; a feature planned for the fair was the Royal Yacht Squadron's Annual Regatta. Subsequently, the RYS offered the Cup as a trophy to the winning yacht in a competition of yachts from all nations. Fifteen yachts (eight cutters and seven schooners) sailed the first race, held at Cowes, on August 22, 1851. The race and the Cup were won by the keel schooner yacht *America*, owned by J.C. Stevens and G.L. Schuyler of New York.

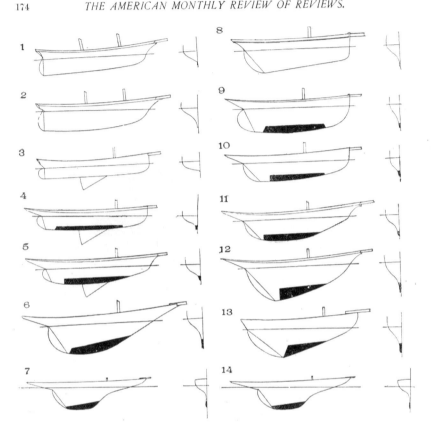

Representative Yacht Profiles, 1848–1895. The dark portion of the sketch represents areas of lead on the keel. American Monthly Review, *August 1899*.

1. *America*, American keel schooner, 1851
2. *Sappho*, American keel schooner, 1867
3. *Mischief*, American centerboard sloop, 1879
4. *Puritan*, American centerboard compromise, 1885
5. *Volunteer*, American centerboard compromise, 1887
6. *Gloriana*, American keel cutter, 1891
7. *Defender*, American keel cutter, 1895
8. *Mosquito*, British keel cutter, 1848
9. *Madge*, British keel cutter, 1879
10. *Galatea*, British keel cutter, 1885
11. *Thistle*, British keel cutter, 1887
12. *Minerva*, British keel cutter, 1888
13. *Glycera*, British keel cutter, 1890
14. *Valkyrie III*, British keel cutter, 1895

The Cup was subsequently offered by its new owners to the New York Yacht Club, subject to certain conditions: that any organized yacht club of any foreign country should forever be entitled to claim the right to sail a match for the Cup, with any vessel that is measured by the customhouse rule of the country to which it may belong; and that the Cup should be the property of the "club" and not the club's members or the owners of the vessel winning it in the match. These conditions, to which others have since been added, are known as the "Deed of Gift."

The trophy is inscribed with names of the yachts that competed in the original regatta, and as additional competitions were played out since 1851, the names of the competitors have been inscribed on the Cup. To accommodate the plethora of engraved names, additional bases matching the Cup's original surface were added in 1958 and 2003.

Beginning in 1887, the eighth match, races have been restricted to two yachts representing, respectively, the challenger and the defender. When, in 1983, the Australian boat, the *Australia II*, wrenched the Cup from the halls of the New York Yacht Club; the longest-running winning streak in the history of sports was broken. Until then, American-designed and American-built boats, crewed by American sailors, had successfully defended the Cup twenty-four times.

Since the first race for possession of the Cup, many millions of dollars and oceans of bad feelings have been expended by challenging and defending yacht clubs. However, advancements in shipbuilding and sailing technology have surged expeditiously by wealthy yachtsmen, marine architects and builders endeavoring to construct the ultimate sailing machine capable of capturing the "Auld Mug."

With the advent of steam-powered ocean cargo carriers after the American Civil War, the use of sailing ships, including the so-called Yankee clippers, otherwise known as the China opium clippers, designers and builders of ocean-going sailing craft needed to find new clientele for their product. Naval architects and wood-and-canvas craftsmen began creating smaller-scale sailboats as upper- and middle-class recreation craft. This is the origin of the sport of sailboat (yacht) racing.

In the late nineteenth century, the most popular type of racing craft were known as sandbaggers. Now known as day sailors, this includes yachts without cabins and no accommodations for crew. These boats are so light that, one hundred years ago, bags of sand were used as ballast; every time the boat tacked, the sandbags shifted. Occasionally, when no sandbags were available, bags of potatoes were chosen for the job. Today, the shifting weight of the crew's bodies act as ballast. Still today, the small early sandbagger class allows people of modest means the ability to enjoy leisurely sailing or pitting one's sailing skill against another by racing.

In order to select the best of the home fleet as a Cup defender, two important principles were introduced into international racing. The time had now come when it was deemed desirable to build a yacht especially for the defense of the Cup, and with this determination, if for no other reason than to tune up and test the new boat, it became necessary to sail a series of trial races.

Up to 1880, the course of yacht modeling in America had run in very even grooves; systematic designing was unknown, and with very few exceptions, yachts were built from small wooden models whittled and carved out by the designer-builders. One type of yacht was in general use: the wide, shoal centerboard craft, with high trunk cabin, large open cockpit, ballast all inside (of iron, or even slag and stone) and a heavy and clumsy wooden construction. Faulty in every way as this type has since been proved, in the absence of any different standard it was considered perfect, and often doubts were expressed of the patriotism if not the sanity of the few American yachtsmen who, about 1877, called into question the merits of the American centerboard sloop and pointed out the opposing qualities of the British cutter—her non-capsizability, due to the use of lead ballast outside of the hull; her speed in rough water; and the superiority of her rig both in proportions and in mechanical details.

Chapter 1
The Deed of Gift

In 1857, the owners of the *America* deeded the Cup to the New York Yacht Club, of which they were members, with the condition that the club place it forever in international competitions. Among other things, the Deed of Gift stated that any foreign yacht club could challenge for a match with a vessel of thirty to three hundred tons. Such a match could be arranged by mutual consent. The Cup became known as the America's Cup and has since been regarded as the symbol of yacht racing supremacy.

In the early years of the competition, the deed was interpreted in a rather one-sided manner. Challengers in the first two matches were met by a multitude of defending yachts. Races were held in lower New York Harbor, where interference from multifarious vessels plying the harbor waters and knowledge of the local waters was advantageous to the defenders.

After the 1881 Cup match, the New York Yacht Club officially returned the Cup to George L. Schuyler, the sole surviving member of the syndicate that owned the *America*, to rewrite the deed to discourage inland-based yacht clubs from challenging the Cup. This revised deed incorporated, among other things, the following rules: the challenger's yacht club's annual regatta must take place on the sea or on the arm of the sea; and the challenging boat must sail to the site of the contest on her own bottom.

In 1887, the challenging yacht's hull was longer than it was originally stated by the challenger; this alarmed the New York Yacht Club, but it rectified the situation by handicapping the challenger. Although the New York Yacht Club successfully defended the Cup that year, it spurred the members to rewrite the deed yet again. Once again the club officially returned the Cup to Mr.

Schuyler. The third deed is much longer and couched in legal terminology; it is unlikely that Mr. Schuyler himself authored the document. The third deed tightened the rules for challenging; for example, it explicitly stated that the challenger must not exceed the dimensions provided to the holder of the Cup. The new version of the rules created uproar among many British yachtsmen, who claimed that the new rules made it impossible to challenge. No one challenged until six years later, when British Lord Dunraven set forth his first of two challenges.

After the Second World War, the New York Yacht Club amended the deed by changing the requirement regarding waterline length: the minimum waterline length was decreased from sixty-five feet to forty-four feet (twenty meters to thirteen meters) to allow the use of the 12-metre class. In addition, the rule that the challenging boat had to sail on her own bottom to the site of the match was eliminated.

In 1985, a second amendment was made to allow for matches to take place during an antipodean summer.[1] The Deed of Gift also allows for a "Mutual Consent Challenge," which allows the races to be conducted under a set of rules that are mutually agreed between the Challenger of Record and the Defender and may differ considerably from the rules as laid down in the Deed of Gift.

According to Halsey C. Herreshoff, the Supreme Court of the State of New York was petitioned by Commodores Henry Sears and Henry Morgan of the New York Yacht Club to change the Deed of Gift.

> *By petitioning the Supreme Court, they modified the Deed of Gift to allow smaller yachts without the previous demand that challengers must cross the ocean on their own bottoms. It was agreed to compete in the International 12-Metre Class, which had provided excellent racing for several years before the war. Designed to the rather tight specifications of the International Rule, these boats did not really fit the grand traditions of the Cup but nevertheless provided nearly three decades of some of the finest match racing ever.*

From time to time over the twentieth century, the deed has been modified: sometimes modestly, sometimes greatly.

In July 1992, the San Diego Yacht Club adapted two interpretive resolutions to the Deed of Gift and an advertising rule to spell out new America's Cup policies regarding sponsor visibility and nationality requirements. Under the advertising rule, advertising on hulls is permitted within rectangular areas up to eight square meters on each side. Advertising on sails is permitted on the mainsail or spinnaker but not on both at the same time. Also, the burgee or initials of the yacht club being represented must be displayed prominently on the transom, no advertising of tobacco products is permitted and the name of the yacht shall not be an advertisement.

The interpretive resolutions prevent sailors and designers from competing with more than one country during a Cup cycle.

Chapter 2
The New York Yacht Club

Before proceeding with discussion of the nuts and bolts of match yacht racing, a short summary of the New York Yacht Club's history is in order. The New York Yacht Club was the second yacht club organized in America, but it has survived the longest.

The first organized yacht club in the United States was the Boston Yacht Club, and that memorable event happened in 1835; its only commodore was Captain R.B. Forbes. Forbes's little schooner, the *Dream*—a tubby, apple-bowed vessel of twenty-eight tons—constituted both fleet and flagship. The club, which went out of existence two years later, was purely a social club for deep-sea fishermen, briny mariners and other salty dowgs with a zest for communal fellowship. The Boston Yacht Club did nothing to foster yacht building or yacht racing. It can only be called a "yacht club" by courtesy and respect to the brave old Boston sailors who were its founders.

On July 30, 1844, a number of wealthy yacht owners who realized the need for an American yachting organization met in the cabin of John C. Stevens's schooner, the *Gimcrack*, anchored off the Battery, and there founded the New York Yacht Club. One of the club's charter members was George L. Schuyler, who captained his schooner the *Dream*, former flagship of the defunct Boston Yacht Club.

The yacht owners present were men of capital and action who, at their founding meeting, elected Mr. Stevens commodore and resolved to sail on their first cruise the next morning. Their destination—Newport, Rhode Island. The little squadron cruised down Long Island Sound, touching at Huntington, New Haven, Gardiner's Bay and Orient Point. Newport was reached on August 5. The village was then only an old-fashioned fishing town with quaint streets and buildings and quainter denizens.

Only sixty-four years after British troops sailed away from Newport, this new friendly invasion of sail drew citizens' attention to the waterfront. Newport was rebuilding from the devastation the British had visited upon it. Scant twenty years earlier, about 1822, Newport was a torpid, quiet place, its trade extinct, its streets deserted; wharves that were once vocal with busy traffic were neglected and sank in pieces under the harbor's water, land had no value and the population had scattered. Strangers rarely found their way to this forgotten old town by the sea; the houses were weather-worn, unpainted and falling to pieces—who would have thought of investing his money in the desolate acres that fringed the borders of this forlorn, dilapidated little village?

No palaces crowned Newport's picturesque heights, no millionaires had yet discovered its marvelous charms. The advent of the squadron was nevertheless an important epoch in the history of the town, which owes its present standing and prosperity to yachtsmen; whose growth has kept pace with that of the New York Yacht Club. Much of Newport's present popularity

The New York Yacht Club Station on Newport Harbor, circa 1910. *Period photo.*

as America's yachting capital is due in part to a former commodore, James Gordon Bennett, who was one of the first young men of wealth to realize the advantages of the harbor and its attractiveness as a summer colony. He was a pioneer of the "cottage"-building frenzy soon to materialize.

The yachts of 1844 would provoke a smile today, but no better amateur sailors manned a halyard or "tailed on" to the end of a mainsheet than the founders of the New York Yacht Club. They wore no uniform or gold braid, they used no pipe to signal commands; there was no military-like etiquette to speak of, beyond the unwritten code that prevails among gentlemen; there was absolutely no red tape. But under their guidance, the sport throve wonderfully and naval architecture was stimulated.

At Newport, the squadron was augmented by the schooner *Northern Light*, owned by Colonel W.P. Winchester of Boston, who had aboard as guest ex-Commodore Forbes, late owner of the *Dream*. These gentlemen and David Sears Jr. joined the club later, being the first Boston yachtsmen who were admitted to membership.

The first annual meeting of the club was held at Windhorst, New York, on March 17, 1845, at which John C. Stevens was reelected commodore. The first clubhouse was built on the Elysian Fields, Hoboken, on a tract of land owned by the Stevens family. It was an unpretentious wood frame structure, a bit dilapidated and weather beaten. As of 1899, this building became the headquarters of the New Jersey Yacht Club.

It was from an anchorage in the Hudson River opposite the Hoboken clubhouse that the start of the first regatta took place on July 17, 1845. At this time, yacht racing was a sport unknown to all but the initiated. However, this particular outing, it is said, drew "thousands of spectators" to the banks of the river. The racecourse was from the clubhouse to the South-west Spit and back. Nine yachts started; the entry fee was five dollars, and the prize was a silver cup bought with the entrance money. It should be remembered that forty-five dollars bought a whole lot more silver in the mid-nineteenth century than it does in the twenty-first century. No doubt the owner of the schooner *Cygnet*, which carried off the cup, was very proud of his victory.

This regatta was the precursor of many historic struggles on the water for modest prizes but, most importantly, for true love of the sport. Commodore Stevens and his fellow yachtsmen were enthusiastic sailors who managed their crafts with the assistance of only a few paid hands, glorying in conflicts with boisterous gales, fitting out their yachts while snow was still blowing and laying them up only out of regret that winter compelled them to do so.

John C. Stevens remained at the post of commodore from 1844 to 1855, when failing health compelled his resignation. He was succeeded by William Edgar, a very able sailor and fair-minded sportsman. Edgar remained at the club's helm until 1860, when Edwin A. Stevens, a brother of the first commodore, was elected. William H. McVickar served in 1866, and Henry G. Stebbins wore the commodore's mantle from 1867 to 1870, when he was replaced by James Gordon Bennett.

Bennett was a sailor yachtsman like none previously known; a resolute daredevil and definite marine eccentric, he was characterized as a top-notch sailor and a thorough sportsman. The annals of the club remember Bennett as liberal, enterprising and lavish with prizes; he owns the distinction of being the only commodore who carried a brass band on his flagship during the annual cruise.

In 1880, the position was held by William H. Thomas for one year; then came John R. Waller and, in 1882, James D. Smith—well known in the financial world as a president of the New York Stock Exchange. Commodore Smith was not unapproachable; rather, he was unpretentious, genial and hearty and in every way a robust sailor. At the time Lord Dunraven challenged for the Cup with his yacht the *Valkyrie*, Commodore Smith exhibited a spirit of hospitality and fair play that was greatly appreciated by the Royal Yacht Squadron.

In 1884, when Sir Richard Sutton challenged for the Cup, Bennett was again elected commodore. Along with Vice-Commodore William P. Douglas, he built the *Priscilla* to defend the Cup. As good as the *Priscilla* was, she was beaten badly by the Boston boat named *Puritan*.

Elbridge T. Gerry came next on the roll of commodores; he served in the position from 1886 to 1892. It is reported that Gerry entertained "sumptuously" on the club's flagship, the *Electra*. Making no pretensions as a sailor, he did prove himself a tolerable steam yachtsman. Not to be outdone by Commodore Bennett's brass band, Commodore Gerry entertained yachting reporters from the leading New York and Boston newspapers on the club's annual cruise. The newspapermen were treated with courtesy and tables groaning from the weight of manly grub, exotic delicacies and alcoholic elixirs—venture to say, all tastes were satisfied. In consequence, the *Electra* was the most widely advertised and popular steam yacht afloat.

When Gerry retired in 1892, in recognition for his many favors to the club, the members presented him with a fine service of silverplate. Commodore Gerry was succeeded by E.D. Morgan, a gentleman who, at the time, had owned more expensive pleasure craft than any other American. As a racing

The New York Yacht Club at Harbour Court, Newport, established 1988.

August 11, 1888: the New York Yacht Club squadron gathered in Newport Harbor. Goat Island and the Naval Torpedo Station can be seen in the right middle ground.

yachtsman, he was singularly unfortunate until he commissioned Nathanael Greene Herreshoff to build the forty-six-foot *Gloriana*, a yacht whose record of eight starts and eight first prizes in New York Yacht Club races was the yachting marvel of 1890.

After the introduction of the *Gloriana* to the New York yacht-racing circuit, the entire course of yacht racing and shape of yacht architecture changed.[2] The victories of the *Gloriana*, coupled with the death of Edward Burgess in 1891, immediately elevated Nat Herreshoff to the forefront of American designers and led to his six successful defenses of the America's Cup.

Chapter 3
Yacht Development
up to the *America*

Althrough the use of sailing vessels for the singular purpose of pleasure was well established in America, it was not until about 1840 that building and racing large oceangoing yachts became common among the country's silk-hatted gentry.

In the mid-nineteenth century, Tobin bronze, steel masts, fin keels and Ratsey sails were unknown, together with numerous other costly refinements of boat building. But the New York Yacht Club was in existence, and it was managed by an enthusiastic and courageous band of wealthy American entrepreneurs who enjoyed their recreational sport of sailing.

During the waning decades of the nineteenth century, yachtsmen complained of the lack of improvement in yacht building since 1850. Up to 1846, American yachting and yacht building may be said to have been in the formative stage. In that year, two brothers, John C. and Edwin A. Stevens, of Hoboken, who about the same time became the most active promoters on the organization of the New York Yacht Club, built the yacht *Maria*, the largest sloop-rigged pleasure craft that had ever been seen afloat up to that time. She was over eighty feet on the waterline and more than one hundred feet overall. She was so large that it was impossible to obtain a single stick to make a boom long and stout enough for her enormous mainsail. So her owners, who were ingenious men, devised a hollow spar made of barrel staves joined together and lashed with iron straps.

From his earliest childhood, John C. Stevens, who may be called the father of the sport of yachting in America, was in love with boats. After building his first nine-foot craft by hand, he built many more that gained in length

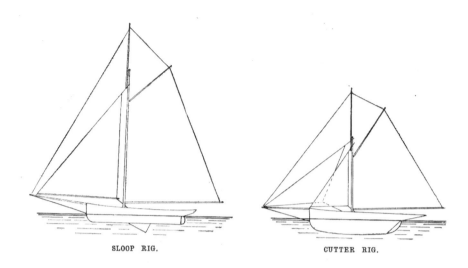

SLOOP RIG.   CUTTER RIG.

Profiles of the American sloop rig and the British cutter rig. Scientific American, *October 14, 1899.*

and weight until he acquired his favorite sloop, the *Maria*. Many yachtsmen of this century agree, in retrospect, that the *Maria* was a half century in advance of her time. Such "modern improvements" included outside lead, a hollow main boom, a heavily weighted main centerboard and a smaller one forward to keep her from falling off in light weather. The *Maria* took to the water in 1844, the year of the founding of the New York Yacht Club.

For a long time, there was the suspicion that George Steers, designer of the *America*, also designed the *Maria*. Writing in the July 1899 issue of *Leslie's Monthly Magazine*, author William E. Simmons assures his readers that through conversations with George L. Schuyler he learned that the *Maria* was designed and built solely by the Stevens brothers. Another source, written by John C. Hemment in an 1899 issue of *Munsey's Magazine*, credits the *Maria*'s model to Robert Livingstone Stevens, the commodore's brother, and construction to William Capes of Hoboken.

The *Maria* beat every competitor she met in American waters so severely that she was originally chosen as the boat to send to England to represent American yachting at the time of the 1851 World's Fair. George Steers, a noted designer and builder of boats with remarkable weatherly and speed qualities, was friendly with the Stevens brothers, the foremost advocates of sending an American yacht to the challenge offered by the Royal Yacht Squadron.

AMERICA, 1851
Designer, GEORGE STEERS
Builder, GEORGE STEERS

The first race for the 100 Guinea Cup was sailed around the Isle of Wight, August 22, 1851. The *America*, built by George Steers for the Stevens brothers, was lying at Cowes; the Stevenses, unable to find a match race, decided to enter the regatta. *Period postcard.*

According to Simmons, Steers made an offer to the Stevens brothers that was difficult to refuse. Steers made the proposition requesting of the brothers the opportunity of designing a boat especially for the purpose of the challenge, and he offered to furnish her rigged and ready to sail free of cost if she did not beat the *Maria*.

Signing on for the $30,000, fully rigged construction of the *America* by George Steers were John C. Stevens, Hamilton Weeks, George L. Schuyler, James Hamilton and J.B. Finlay. After the model was approved by the syndicate, the *America* was built at the William H. Brown shipyard up the East River at the foot of Twelfth Street. The *America*, 101 feet 9 inches overall, 94 feet on deck, 90 feet waterline and 22 feet beam, drew 11 feet of water; her mainmast was 81 feet long, and her foremast was over 79 feet; both masts strongly raked. Her bowsprit was 32 feet long from tip to heel, and her main boom was 53 feet, swinging well out past her stern—exceptional lengths. Gaff-rigged, she was modeled on the New York Harbor pilot boat model, carrying neither foretopmast nor jib boom. Steers followed the same sharp bow lines and slim hull that he had developed and built so successfully.

Before the days of wireless communication between ship and shore, there was great competition between pilot boat captains; therefore, speed was a particularly favorable quality for a pilot boat. Typically, pilots headed out to sea in the early morning looking for sailing craft that needed an escort into the harbor. These pilot boats were fit for all weather conditions, they had to be seaworthy and it was necessary to be of shallow draft.

While the *America* was built mostly along the lines of a pilot schooner for speed, her below decks were a combination of efficiency and comfort for crew. Her sail locker stood under the cockpit, and her main saloon occupied the space from her mainmast, aft. Six berths were built around the sides of the saloon; forward of the mainmast were four staterooms, the galley, a pantry and a forecastle with fifteen berths and a toilet; there also were clothes and storage lockers occupying the length of the passageway from the saloon to the cockpit.

While the yachts of both nations were still of the (so-called) "cod's head and mackerel's tail" model formerly considered indispensable to speed, Steers had for some years experimented in exactly the opposite direction, making the bows very fine and the stern proportionately fuller. With this difference in model was a corresponding one in the cut of the *America*'s sails, which were made to sit as flat as possible, while those of the opposing fleet were cut, according to the prevailing theories, with an extravagant amount of fullness or "bag."[3]

The Cup's namesake, the *America*, in post–Civil War rig. *Photo from the* Century Magazine, *August 1893.*

When the *America* came out and sailed against the *Maria*, she was beaten so badly that the syndicate almost relinquished the idea of sending her over. Today, we understand that nineteenth-century yachtsmen failed to recognize the fact that a large sloop, being able to sail closer than a schooner, will invariably beat her in windward work and generally to such an extent as to prevent the superiority of the schooner with lifted sheets from recovering lost ground.

The only craft that could beat the *America* in her trial races, preliminary to her voyage across the Atlantic to England in 1851, was the *Maria*, of which it is written, "sailed 'round her with ridiculous ease." So decisive was the victory of the sloop over the schooner that Commodore Stevens and his associates doubted it would be advisable to send the *America* across to compete against the British.

After her first trial, the *America* was somewhat improved, but she was never able to hold her own against the *Maria*. However, the *America* beat every other craft she sailed against; therefore, the Stevens brothers and their associates decided to pay Steers for the boat and send her to England.

The *America*'s performance in the Solent is too well known to be recounted here. However, suffice to say that after sailing across the Atlantic and fitting out at Havre in early August, the *America* beat a path to Cowes, arriving on a dark night. It must have been an interesting moment when the dawn showed her to the great fleet of English boats full of yachtsmen straining their eyes to size up the Yankee stranger. With her great beam and shallow hull, the *America* was as different from the English as squirrels are from sparrows.

After the Cup presentation, Stevens sailed the *America* in British waters for a time before selling her to Lord John deBlaquiere, who later cut down her masts by five feet and used her chiefly for cruising in his home waters. The amputated rig proved to be a failed operation because the *America* never performed as well as she did with her original rig. In 1861, she again changed owners when she was sold to a Lord Templeton, who changed her name to *Camilla* and used her for pleasure cruising for about one year; becoming weary of her, his Lordship laid her up in the mud at Cowes, where she languished, rotting for four years. At the end of that time, she was refloated and restored at the Northfleet yards using English oak; she eventually reappeared sturdier than when initially launched.

In 1860, Henry Decie became the new owner and raced her successfully in a few races. In 1861, Decie sailed her to Savannah, Georgia, just in time for the beginning of hostilities between Confederate and Union forces. In October 1861, the yacht was sold to a Southern gentleman with Confederate sympathies who changed her name to *Memphis*. In Savannah, she was fitted out as a Confederate gunboat armed with one big gun. Her altered rig

MAGIC, 1870
Designer, R. F. LOPER
Builders, THOMAS BYERLY & SON

In the 1870 challenge, the British schooner *Cambria* raced against an American fleet of fifteen yachts; she placed tenth, the *Magic* took the Cup and the *America*, now fourteen years old, placed fourth. *Period postcard.*

caused her speed to greatly decrease, so she was useless as a blockade runner. She served as a dispatch courier for several months until one day she was chased up the St. John's River in Florida, where, in order to avoid capture, she was scuttled without ceremony.

After lying in the mud for several months, she was raised by the crew of the Union frigate *Wabash* (another source says the Union ship *Ottawa*) and next saw service with the fleet blockading Charleston. She later aided in the capture of several Confederate ships. In 1864, the well-used *America* was retired from service as a warship and became a training vessel for Annapolis cadets.

When James Ashbury brought his schooner yacht *Cambria* to New York in 1870, the tired old *America* was refitted as a yacht by the U.S. Navy, and she took part in the race, along with twenty-two others, against the *Cambria*. Still speedy in her dotage, the *America* finished at two hours, fifteen minutes, twenty-five seconds, in fourth behind the winner *Magic* (two hours, five minutes, sixteen seconds) and ahead of the eighth-place finisher, the challenger *Cambria*, at two hours, twenty-seven minutes, nineteen seconds.

After the race, the *America* was purchased at auction by General Benjamin F. Butler, who gave her an overhanging stern and outside lead and otherwise altered her along modern lines, making her, in John C. Hemment's words, "looking quite young and handsome."

Chapter 4

Schooners, Sloops and Cutters

The shallow bays with which United States' coasts abound encouraged development of a type of yacht, light of draft and broad of beam, particularly suitable for estuarial cruising. There came about a notable difference in the accepted types of schooners and sloops. Typically, the American schooner is a boat having two or more masts, all fore- and-aft rigged. In the case of the two-masted schooner, the after mast must be at least as high as the forward one. Schooners were used chiefly for deep-sea cruising; they were built of deeper draft and less beam in proportion to their length. Thus, there were many keel schooners, including the *America*, *Dauntless* and *Sappho*. The sloop is a single-masted boat with one sail aft of the mast and one or more jibs forward; prior to 1882, a keel sloop was almost unknown. In that year, however, several single stickers, built on the English cutter model, made their appearance, but they mostly failed to win races. This type of cutter was largely abandoned.

The big sloops that won prizes, the *Fanny*, *Mischief* and *Gracie*, all beamy, light draft, centerboard yachts, also won high places in the esteem of American yachtsmen. Of these three sloops named as contenders for the first honor of defending the Cup in the 1880s, the *Fanny* represented the extreme "skimming-dish" type and the *Gracie* a more moderate embodiment of beam with greater draft. In light breezes and smooth water, the *Fanny* was generally the victor, while in strong winds and rough seas, the *Gracie* invariably captured the prize. The *Mischief*, an intermediate between the two, was a dangerous adversary in light or moderate weather.

SAPPHO, 1871, *leading*
  Designer, RICHARD POILLON
  Builders, POILLON BROS.

In this artist's representation, the keel schooner *Sappho* is leading the British keel cutter yacht *Livonia* in the fourth race of the 1871 series. *Period postcard.*

COLUMBIA, 1871
  Designer, J. B. VANDEUSEN
  Builder, J. B. VANDEUSEN

The New York Yacht Club's centerboard yacht, the *Columbia*, won two of the first three races against the *Livonia*. *Period postcard.*

The 1876 race was between the Canadian *Countess of Dufferin* and the *Madeleine*. The *Madeleine* soundly beat the Canadian in two races. *Period postcard.*

In 1881, Canada sent down a challenge with the sloop *Atalanta*. The *Mischief* won both matches by considerable margins. *Period postcard.*

The *Mischief* was eventually selected to defend the Cup in 1881 against the Canadian challenger, the *Atalanta*. The Canadian was beaten so badly as to give a decidedly farcical aspect to the effort of our friendly neighbors. Both matches were won by the *Mischief* without a bit of trouble, the first by thirty-one minutes and fourteen and a half seconds and the second by forty-one minutes and thirty-nine seconds, actual time.

At the time, it was claimed by many that England had several boats that could have beaten both the challenger and the defender; but England did not know it, and America would not admit it.

As a result of the sloop and cutter controversy, there was sent out to New York in the fall of 1881 the little ten-ton racing cutter the *Madge*, one of the most successful of her class on the Clyde—a deep, narrow, lead-keeled craft with the typical cutter rig. She was owned by Mr. James Coats, of Paisley, Scotland, and his object in sending her to America was to test the type against the American sloop. The *Madge* sailed in five races at New York and two at Newport, winning all but one, in which she was beaten by the *Shadow*, a famous Herreshoff sloop of more than the usual depth. She also beat the *Shadow* in one of the races at Newport. The success of the *Madge* was encouraging to the cutter contingent, and not a little confusing to their opponents, but the battle of depth, low weight and cutter rig was by no means won; there was plenty of fight still left in the sloop group. With the building of the *Bedouin*, a seventy-foot cutter, in 1882, the fight went on with renewed vigor..The cutter cause was hindered at times by the failure of some of the larger ones built here but gained gradually as the problem became better understood of adapting to American conditions the leading principles of the cutter type, and also as the owners of such cutters as the *Bedouin* and *Oriva* came to know their boats better and to work them up to racing form. From the performances of the *Bedouin* with the *Gracie* and *Mischief*, it was demonstrated that the modified cutter of moderate beam was at least the equal of the wide centerboard sloop.

Although no more sloops were built after the failure of the *Pocahontas* in 1881, several new cutters of large size were added to the British fleet each year, and 1884 saw the launch of two, the *Genesta* and *Irex*. Following the natural course of designing under the old tonnage rule, with its heavy restriction on beam, each of these was a little narrower, deeper and longer than the existing boats of the class, with greater displacement and sail area, the *Genesta* being eighty-one feet waterline, fifteen feet beam, thirteen feet six inches draft, and the *Irex* being three feet longer with the same beam and draft. At the end of the season, the *Genesta* had shown herself rather better than the *Irex*, and her owner, Sir Richard Sutton, decided to challenge for the America's Cup. Another British yachtsman, Lieutenant William Henn, RN, an old sailor and deepwater cruiser, had long entertained the same ambition. Encouraged by the *Genesta*'s success in her first season, he ordered a yacht from the same designer, Mr. J. Beavor Webb.[4]

Early in January 1885, two simultaneous challenges were received from England and accepted. A series was arranged for 1885 with the *Genesta* owned by Sir Richard Sutton and another series with the *Galatea* owned by Lieutenant Henn for 1886. Two races were planned for each of these matches.

The challenge of the *Genesta* was received by the New York Yacht Club through the Royal Yacht Squadron. The keel cutter *Genesta* had defeated, with somewhat ease, the swiftest craft of her kind in British waters. American yachtsmen quickly recognized that there was no sloop yet afloat in American waters that could hope successfully to meet the challenger.

This English challenge was instrumental in the forming of two American syndicates, each with the goal of building a superior Cup defender.

Early in 1885, five members of Boston's Eastern Yacht Club, notable among whom were Vice-Commodore J. Malcolm Forges, General Charles J. Paine and Secretary Edward Burgess, met and drafted their plan for building a boat for the defense of the Cup. Their plan was to use more advanced and scientific ideas than those currently in use by any sloop afloat.

The Boston syndicate contracted Edward Burgess, a young Boston designer of scientific training, who had turned out some fast cats and other small boats but nothing as yet along the lines of a large racing sloop. The result of Burgess's design was the *Puritan*, a radical departure from all existing yachts.

To say the *Puritan* was a departure from the accepted type is probably an understatement. The relation of *Puritan*'s beam to length had been, in round numbers, as one to three, while in her it was reduced to one to four. There was a slight increase in her actual draft, though the relation of draft to waterline length was somewhat less than that of the *Gracie*. The latter—with a waterline length 69 feet 3½ inches—drew 8 feet, while the former—with 81.1 feet waterline—drew only 8 feet 10 inches. It was in the disposition of the ballast, however, that the *Puritan* differed radically from any sloop previously built on typical American lines before this. This was run into a strip of lead 45 feet long, 2 feet wide and 16 inches thick and bolted on the outside of her keel. It weighed 48 tons. She also had a nine-hundred-pound shoe on the foot of her centerboard. The *Gracie*, the *Fanny* and other racing sloops carried pig iron between their ribs for ballast, but in this instance,

For the sixth race for the Cup, in 1885, the British sloop *Genesta* proved herself a marvel of speed. Sir Richard Sutton was told he could sail the course over and have the Cup, the *Puritan* having been disqualified for fouling. Sutton declined, and thus the Cup stayed with the New York Yacht Club. *Period stereoview card.*

besides a great increase of ballast, there was a concentration of it below the keel, with the result of an important gain in stability. The idea of placing ballast below the keel was borrowed from the English, who had long used it.

The *Puritan*, with her straight stem, high bows and long stern overhang, differed so greatly in appearance from her sister sloops that she had little "sex appeal" to the eyes of New York yachtsmen. Author William E. Simmons writes upon viewing her in New London, "She was really a handsome vessel, being a fine embodiment of power, and after showing what she could do, speedily came to be regarded as such."

About the same time, New York Yacht Club commodore James Gordon Bennett and Vice-Commodore William P. Douglas commissioned Mr. A.

Cary Smith, a New York designer, to build a new sloop for the coming defense of the Cup. The New York boat was the *Priscilla*, in reality an enlarged *Mischief*.

With the exception of the *Mischief*, which was an iron boat, the preceding defenders were all wooden boats. The *Priscilla* was a centerboard sloop with a hull of iron, but she did not come up to the standard of the *Puritan*, and wood, therefore, continued to be preferred.

After a series of competitive races, the *Puritan* was selected to defend the Cup.

The *Genesta* was a typical "Thames measurement" deep keel cutter, eighty-one feet on the water line, fifteen feet beam and thirteen feet, six inches draught. The *Puritan* was a marked departure from the other Americans of her genre, of which she retained only the characteristic features of great beam, shallow hull and centerboard. She carried the cutter rig practically in its entirety and also forty-eight tons of lead at the foot of her keel. With a displacement smaller than that of the *Genesta*, by some thirty-six tons, she carried a slightly larger sail spread.

In the first race, for the sixth defense, which came off on September 14, 1885, the *Puritan* fouled the *Genesta* in an attempt to cross her bow when the latter boat had the right of way. The committees immediately ruled the *Puritan* out and gave the race to the *Genesta* with the privilege of sailing the course over and having the Cup. In a supreme gesture of good sportsmanship, Sir Richard Sutton refused the privilege, thereby setting a precedent that may well have governed all such future unfortunate contingencies.

However, regardless of the committee's granting the race to the British yacht, in a light and fluky wind, the shallow, light displacement boat won easily by sixteen minutes and nineteen seconds.

The second race resulted in one of the most exciting and memorable contests in the history of the struggle for the Cup. The course was twenty miles to leeward and return, and the *Genesta* rounded the outer mark fully an eighth of a mile ahead. On the twenty-mile close-hauled run to the home mark, the wind freshened and offered a wonderful opportunity to test the windward qualities of the two types of vessel. The *Puritan*, seeing the probability of an increase in the strength of the wind, took in her topsail and housed her topmast; but the cutter, clinging to her topsail and heeling down to the wind until the forty-eight tons of lead in her keel could get in their steadying effect, began to make a fine exhibition of cutter work in the favorable cutter weather. The *Puritan* under her snugger canvas, and with the incomparable centerboard to edge her up into the wind, began steadily to overhaul her challenger, and sailing up into the weather berth, she came galloping home the winner of a magnificent race by the close margin of one minute and thirty-eight seconds.

The sloop *Genesta* proved herself a marvel of speed, and although beaten in both races by the *Puritan*, she went on to win the Cape May and Brenton's Reef Cups.

The following year, the seventh race, and the sixth challenge, witnessed races between the cutter *Galatea* and the centerboard sloop the *Mayflower*, which, like the *Puritan*, was owned by General Payne of Boston. After the decisive defeat of the *Genesta* by the *Puritan*, little apprehension was entertained regarding the visit of the *Galatea*, because she was known to be an inferior vessel to her predecessor.

In several important respects, the *Mayflower* differed essentially from the *Puritan*. She had greater waterline length, less proportional beam, more draft, more ballast and a larger sail area. The sail is to the yacht what the engine is to the steamer, and all modifications of hull have for their ultimate end increase of sail area. The *Puritan* had 832 square feet more sail area than the *Genesta*, and the *Mayflower* had 652 square feet more sail area than the *Puritan*.

The *Galatea* did not differ essentially from the *Genesta* except in size. She was a larger boat; however, we have read that she was "not nearly so handsome." Although a leaner vessel, her lines were not as fine. She had within a fraction of 6 feet more on her waterline length with the same beam, 15 feet, and half a foot more draft, eight tons more ballast and 355 square feet more sail area.

The first match was won easily by the centerboard sloop; the *Mayflower* embarrassed the British keel cutter by winning by twelve minutes and two seconds. In the second race, there was so little wind that the *Mayflower* barely made the course in the time allowed but eventually won by twenty-nine minutes and nine seconds, leaving her opponent far behind.

The *Galatea* afterward proved herself a very able cruising yacht. As in the case of Sir Richard Sutton, Lieutenant Henn, owner of the *Galatea*, became well liked through his unfailing good nature and sportsmanship.

Soon after the *Mayflower* whipped the *Galatea* so severely, the New York Yacht Club received notice from the Royal Clyde Yacht Club of a challenge for the succeeding year. This challenger, the *Thistle*, was the first to show the influence of the Cup matches on English yacht building. For the first time since 1871, a yacht was built in England for the specific purpose of capturing the America's Cup. The *Thistle* was a radical departure from the cutter type. The English, after a number of embarrassing defeats by Yankee sloops, had abandoned their old designs and leaned toward the Yankee model.

In 1886, Lieutenant Henn brought his *Galatea* over to face off against the Edward Burgess–designed and George Lawley & Son–built *Mayflower*. *Period postcard.*

While Yankee marine architects had modified their ideas of the superlative importance of beam and come to recognize the value of draft, the English were forced to acknowledge potency of draft as a factor of speed.

The realization of the impossibility of winning the Cup with a yacht built under the restrictions of the Thames rule of measurement led to the adoption of a new rating rule based on water length and sail area; this resulted in a return to the broader beam that had characterized the earlier English cutters of the *Mischief* type. The effect was noticeable in the next challenger, the Scottish yacht the *Thistle*. The *Thistle*, with a fraction of a foot less length on the waterline than the *Galatea*, had over five feet more abeam. The singular most important result was that with 70 tons ballast—10 tons fewer than the *Galatea*—and not quite three inches more draft and 138 tons displacement, she was able to carry 1,463 square feet more sail; except for her teak deck, she was fully steel constructed. The *Thistle* beat everything in English waters that dared to challenge her so decisively that the jubilant Scotchmen had no doubt that they would capture the Cup.

As soon as the dimensions of the *Thistle* were received on this side of the Atlantic, General Paine and Mr. Burgess began construction of a new sloop, with a view to improving on the *Mayflower*. With his newly designed

The British cutter *Genesta*, of 1884–85 (left), and the *Galatea*, 1885 (right). *Photo from the* Century Magazine, *August 1893.*

Volunteer, Edward Burgess had his third triumph with two decisive wins over Scotland's *Thistle*.

From 1888 to 1890, the *Thistle* had a superb racing career in British waters. In 1891, she was sold to Emperor Wilhelm II for 90,000 gold marks. She was renamed *Meteor* and became the Kaiser's racing yacht. The *Meteor* was the first yacht registered on the Imperial German Yacht Club lists, founded at Kiel in 1891; she regularly raced in Cowes.

Chapter 5
Points and Paces of Sailing Yacht Racers

A racing yacht is high-strung, fragile and beautiful; it is created with the single goal of achieving great speed. Generally, the lighter the yacht and the greater the spread of sail, the greater will be the speed.

However, a boat too light will not be strong enough to support the immense square footage of its engines—its sails; it is the genius of the designer who must find its perfect work in approaching closest to this deadline ratio between lightness and strength. The very fact that every portion of the yacht has been pared down to its finest is a stern warning to the racing enthusiast that he must keep a sharp eye for accidents. For instance, a *Columbia*-type yacht upon her trial and tuning run could snap its huge steel mast like a twig; a broken gaff will douse the mainsail of a racer in the midst of a match.

To ensure the necessary lightness, Captain Nat Herreshoff built *Columbia* of the metal known as Tobin bronze, which at the time was a fairly new lightweight alloy. The thickness of this plating material varies from one-quarter to three-sixteenths inch. Besides lightness, one of the greatest assets of using Tobin bronze for the yacht's hull is that it is not affected by seawater and requires no paint; consequently, the yacht's bottom will be shiny and smooth, allowing less friction and easier slippage through the water.

Before the *Columbia*, Captain Nat built the *Defender*'s hull with aluminum. This metal, exceedingly expensive in 1895, weighs only half as much as bronze and is stronger by half; but it was found in the *Defender* that salt water causes rapid corrosion and deterioration of aluminum.

One of the greatest wonders of the late nineteenth-century and early twentieth-century racing yachts is the ability of a seventy-ton body to support a great slab of lead on its keel weighing more than ninety tons and fifteen or twenty tons of rigging, sails and a crew of thirty to fifty hands.

Chapter 6 explains the most salient details of the inner-body supports of the classic period America's Cup yacht.

Technical information for the following section is from an article by Ray Stannard Baker, "The Racing Yacht: Its Points and Its Paces," in *McClure's Magazine*, October 1899.

THE KEEL AND ITS LEAD BALLAST

No question in yacht building is quite as interesting and important as the one concerning the keel. The centerboard is a loose keel-board that drops down sideways through a slit in the bottom of the boat, or a fin keel that cuts deep like the fin of a fish, or an ordinary deep cutter keel. The famous old defenders, the *Volunteer* and the *Puritan*, were centerboards, a favorite of American yachtsmen, whereas later yachts such as the *Defender* and the *Columbia*, and all the English racers, have sported the deep keel.

Before about 1873, racers were ballasted with pigs of lead or iron stowed in the hold; since then, the finer yachts have all depended on what is called

In this photograph, the *Volunteer*'s crew is setting the jib-topsail. *Photo from the* Century Magazine, *August 1893.*

The new cutter yacht *Thistle*, built to compete with the American yachts for the America's Cup.

"outside ballast," meaning the weight of lead attached to the keel. This weight prevents the yacht from being pried out of the water when the wind strikes her beam or side. For this reason, the skipper is enabled to spread a big sail even in a heavy blow, where a boat of lesser draft and lighter keel load would be all but blown out of the water. The *Columbia*, with her enormous lead keel, was said to be a "stiff sailor"; in other words, she stood up well in a brisk wind. It appears that the sailor with the heavy lead keel, the least wetted surface and a superior tactician should win every race he enters.

These two fine points of the winning racer—the light hull and the deep, heavy keel—were made more effective in the *Columbia* by a wonderful economy and beauty of design. Captain Nat Herreshoff carved *Columbia*'s curves with the grace of the arched back and pointed toes of a ballet dancer. Before computer design technology, designers such as Captain Nat whittled their models from a block of wood and tried it according to the pleasure of their eye, and it often happened that after a vessel was finished it needed to be, unavoidably, carved away at one point and thickened at another in order to remedy vital sailing defects.

John Brown Herreshoff puts a hand on his latest America's Cup yacht, naming her *Defender*; his brother Nathanael Greene Herreshoff approves.

Today, yacht modeling is much more science, superior technology and computer-generated graphics. Large, powerful computers like the Cray Supercomputer have pushed the envelope of yacht designing to extremes never dreamed of by early and mid-twentieth-century designers. The designer of the classic yachts knew, as today's designers know, the curve of displacement with mathematical certainty, and he can float his yacht exactly on a predetermined waterline. But the genius of a modern Burgess or Herreshoff may still find play in shaping the beautiful curves of the hull, for in that particular yacht designing is still an art and always will be, no matter what the contemporary aid may be.

One of the greatest advancements made in the development of the hull of the racing yacht has come chiefly through the Herreshoffs and that company's first great sailing yacht, the *Gloriana*. That advancement was in cutting away the bulk of the vessel under the water. The hull of the *Columbia*, for instance, was about 90 feet long where it met the surface of the water, whereas her total length overall was more than 131 feet; in other words, about 41 feet was "overhang" at bow and stern. The object of this cutting away at bow and stern and on the sides leaves the racing yacht with hardly more of a hold than a catboat. This marvelous idea of cutting away is primarily to reduce the area of friction, although the overhang has its own special and important purpose. When a yacht is beaten over to one side during the heat of a race, the overhanging portions of the hull come into contact with the water and prevent further tipping, thereby adding greatly to the quality of the vessel's "stiffness." The overhang forward is also of great assistance in bringing up the yacht when she is plunging and ascending through high waves.

The *Gloriana* at the finish in the 1891 Goelet Cup race.

Rigging and Sails

In all cases, the rigging and sails of a great racing yacht are equally as important as hull and keel. The Cup challengers and defenders since the *Atalanta* challenged the *Mischief* in 1881 have been sloop-rigged; that is, they have had a single mast. The original Cup winner, the *America*, was a schooner—a double masted boat, also known as a "two-sticker." The first steel mast ever employed on a Cup defender was on the *Columbia*—a great steel tube, made of plates and braced inside with angle irons. Above it rose the topmast, 64 feet long, and above that the club-topsail pole, so that the highest tip of the yacht was 175 feet above the water (35 feet too high to pass under the Brooklyn Bridge) and 44 feet more than the length of the yacht. The exact location of this great length of metal, so that the center of lateral resistance of the hull and the sails will be exactly balanced, is the last and most important secret that the builder has to divulge. In reality, there is no strict rule regarding placement of the mast; the designer must rely on the wise dictates of his experience. To provide the requisite strength of the mast-step for a mighty yacht such as the *Columbia* is explained in Chapter 6.

The yacht's rigging is largely of flexible wire rope, and the halyards (ropes that are used to lift the sails) are of metal, with manila cords artfully spliced to their handling ends.

For the uninitiated, it is difficult to realize the immense spread of the *Columbia*'s canvas. The steel boom that stretches the foot of her mainsail is nearly 110 feet long, exceeding by 20 feet the waterline length of the yacht herself, so that, when "close hauled" (when the boom is drawn in until it is nearly parallel with the length of the boat), the tip extends far out over the water to the rear of the yacht. It is calculated that *Columbia*'s 15,000-square-foot sail was the largest sail ever placed on a vessel of any size at that time. All the sails, except the spinnaker and the balloon jib-topsail, were of the very finest cotton duck. This fabric was treated with a chemical solution of French origin that purportedly made the cloth airtight.

Making sails for the classic Cup yachts was undertaken in the same scientific way the rest of the yacht was created. Consider the architecture required for these sails so that they would curve and catch the wind like a bird's wing, drawing perfectly yet without wrinkling or straining the canvas. There is a degree of art and accuracy not easily appreciated without a visit to a sailmaker's loft.

Up to 1885 when the *Genesta* came seeking the Cup, the English had used hempen, a tough Asian fiber, for their sails. The English yachtsmen of the

When the *Genesta* came over in search of the Cup in 1885, the *Puritan*, designed by Edward Burgess, was the defender.

Genesta returned home without the Cup but did take a sample of the material of which American sails were made. Since then, American cotton has been the preferred material widely adopted by all grades of British ships, as well as the American system of attaching the sails to spars.

When the racing yacht is launched and rigged and the sails properly fitted, the designer and the builder have done their utmost to bring that vessel to victory. From this point, the yacht's owner and his skipper must take the fragile craft in their knowing hands and sail her to victory.

In each succeeding Cup race, more tireless attention has been given to the selection of the crew. In 1895, veteran skipper Captain Hank Haff went to Maine to handpick a crew of native-born Yankee seamen to man the *Defender*. The *Defender* sailed to victory, and her crew drew praise for their coolness, precision and knowledge of sail handling. These massive racing yachts required thirty to fifty men to handle their enormous sails, enough of a crew to crowd the narrow deck until it has the appearance of an excursion boat and enough of a weight to help appreciably in crushing down a windward beam in a squall.

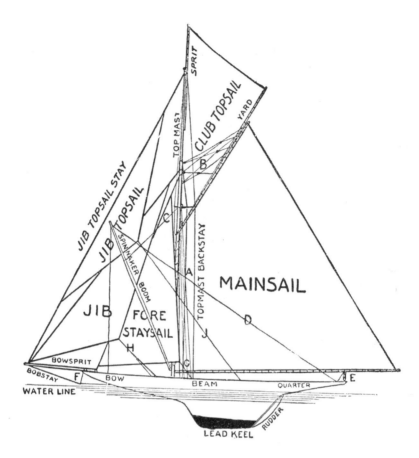

A diagram of the modern (1899) racing yacht. A. shrouds; B. peak halyards; C. spinnaker boom; D. spinnaker sheet; E. main sheet; F. martingale; G. fore-staysail; H. jib-sheet; J. jib-topsail sheet. *Graphic from* McClure's Magazine, *October 1899.*

POINTING

The modern racing yacht is expected to be equally proficient in all of her paces. The chief of these is called "pointing," which expresses the ability of the yacht to sail in the direction from which the wind is blowing. All sailing craft, when the wind is dead ahead of them, are compelled to tack back and forth, and the vessel that can make its course with the fewest tacks—that is, sail the straightest toward the wind—will probably win the race. The *Columbia*, for instance, could point her bowsprit well within four points, or forty-five degrees of the wind, closer, perhaps, than

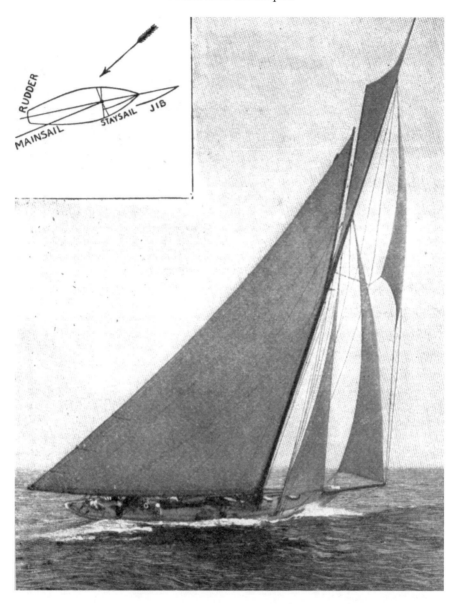

The *Columbia* pointing, or sailing toward the wind. In pointed, the mainsail is "close hauled"—that is, drawn in almost parallel with the yacht. The crew is lying well up toward the windward to keep the yacht balanced. The arrow in this and succeeding diagrams marks the direction of the wind. McClure's Magazine, *October 1899*.

any American yacht in the classic era of Cup competition. In pointing, the sheets (the ropes that let out or pull in the boom and control the mainsail) are hauled in close so that the boom is almost parallel with the length of the yacht; and if the wind is strong, the racer often lies over until her lee rails (the side of the yacht away from the wind) are awash, and the men lie up to the windward flat on their sides like rows of dried herring. A yacht in this trim is said to be "close hauled."

REACHING

The next most important pace of the yacht is called "reaching," in which she is said to be sailing with "started sheets." This means that her boom is allowed to swing a little outboard, at an acute angle with the length of the yacht, so that the mainsail catches a good deal of the breeze. In reaching, the wind is on one side, or beam, of the yacht, or just abaft of the beam; that is, toward the stern.

RUNNING

The third pace of the racer is called "running," in which the wind is blowing directly behind the yacht. In this case the sheets are "eased away," or let out, until the mainsail stands at a broad angle with the length of the boat. It is in running before the wind that the yachtsman "breaks out" or spreads his spinnaker, the spinnaker being an exceedingly important racing sail that is set by means of a removable boom, just opposite the balancing of the mainsail. It is an enormous sail of light balloon cloth. A good yacht's crew can put up the spinnaker boom and break out the great sail within five minutes. It is always the occasion of great activity and excitement aboard the vessel, and he is a wise slipper who knows just the proper moment to put up and take down his spinnaker.

Landlubbers, as we are, quite likely think that a yacht makes its best speed when running before the wind, but that is not necessarily the case. Let us consider the *Columbia*; she could make more speed by several knots when reaching than when running before the wind. That is interesting! Here is the relatively simple answer: with the wind astern, only her mainsail and spinnaker, with possibly a topsail and one forward sail, are filled and drawing, whereas while she is reaching she spreads her full canvas—mainsail, topsail,

The yacht *Vigilant* is reaching. In reaching, the wind is on the yacht's beam, and were it not for the deep keel with its heavy lead load, she might be blown over. The "sheets" are let out until the mainsail makes a sharp angle with the boat. The rudder, if moved at all, is set to the lee to keep the yacht well up to the wind. In this illustration, the racing top—the big light club-topsail—owing to the evident force of the wind is not in use; the forestaysail and the jib are all spread. McClure's Magazine, *October 1899*.

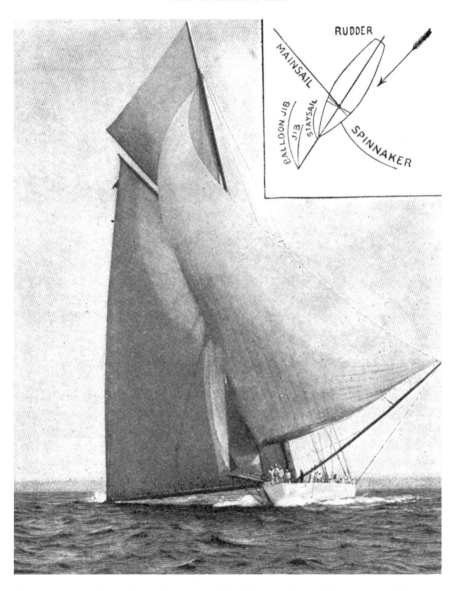

Here, the *Defender* is running before the wind. In this pace, the wind is straight behind.
Two broad wings, the mainsail on the left and the spinnaker on the right, balloon with the
following wind. At the top, the triangular club-topsail is spread. Between the two wings,
a little jib and a forestaysail are set to catch wind spilled from the greater sails. The crew
stands about in such positions that their backs will catch the wind and so help the sails.
McClure's Magazine, *October 1899.*

forestaysail, jib and jib-topsail—provided the wind is not too heavy. A racer will sometimes make as high as fourteen knots while reaching.

There are several important sails used on a racing yacht that do not appear on an ordinary pleasure cruising yacht. The typical sloop rig consists of a big mainsail, a forestaysail, a jib, a topsail and jib-topsails of two or three sizes. In addition to this full complement of canvas, the racer has a spinnaker, a balloon jib-topsail and a club-topsail. The balloon jib-topsail, which is an enormous sail made of soft light cloth, is spread at the extreme bow of the boat when the wind is light. It will often drive a large-hulled racer at considerable speed when there is apparently not a breath of a breeze. The club-topsail is a large, light, triangular sail that occupies the place of the ordinary topsail but spreads far above and beyond it. If we continue using the *Columbia* as an example, the "sprit," or the longer of the two club-topsail poles on which the club-topsail is spread, is fifty-eight feet in length. This enormous spread of sail is only used to catch light winds, and the skipper must keep a sharp lookout for squalls, otherwise he may have his racing top blown away and totally lost.

As in all yacht races, the courses are planned to give the competitors the greatest possible variety of sailing weather—the greater the challenge, the greater the victory.

Chapter 6
Anatomy of a Classic Cup Yacht

O ur old standby for information about early America's Cup yachts' defending and challenging campaigns for the Cup, the weekly *Scientific American* in its May 11, 1901 edition published a long and detailed article titled "Principles of Design." From my research on the subject, I find this to be one of the finest, most informative and easily understood articles on the subject of the classic period of ocean racing yacht design. This article disseminates all the literal "nuts and bolts" of large ocean-racing sailboats.

PRINCIPLES OF DESIGN

Other things being equal, the fundamental object aimed at in the design of a 90-foot racing yacht is power, or the ability to carry a maximum amount of sail. This may be secured by changes of form or by [reduction of] or [moving] of weights, or both. Increased power due to form is gained by increase of beam, by flattening the floor and "hardening" or filling out the bilges, thereby raising the center of buoyancy and placing the body of the boat more upon the surface of the water. Power due to form, however, is gained at the expense of sweetness of lines and ease of propulsion: hence the genius of the designer is shown in finding that happy mean which gives a maximum power with a minimum hardness of form. Thus, comparing the last three Herreshoff boats, Defender *presents in her midship section the sweetest and most beautiful form ever seen in an American 90-footer, the bilges rounding in to the reverse curve of the garboards with the unbroken sweep of a letter* S. *In* Columbia *the floor is flatter, the beam is increased, the bilge hardens and the garboard curve is reduced. In* Constitution *the development has been pushed still further: there is even less floor and the bilge is still harder than that of* Columbia. *The results of this development, in terms of sail area are seen in the respective figures of 12,640 square feet for* Defender, *13,125 square feet for* Columbia, *and 14,400 for* Constitution.

Olin Stephens (left) and Starling Burgess (right) form the *Ranger*'s crack designing team.

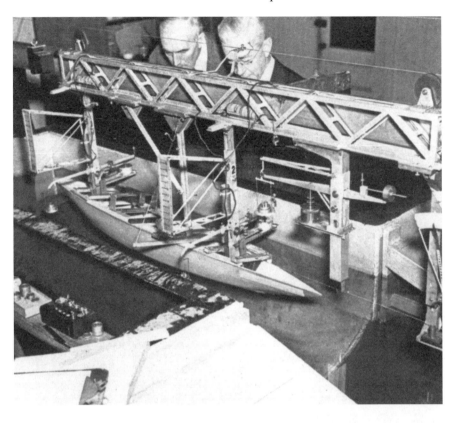

Above: Scale models of the *Ranger* were built and tested in a one-hundred-foot tank at Stevens Institute of Technology. *Ranger* models were "raced" against a model of the *Endeavour*.

Right: From the wooden pattern, seen in this photo, a sand mold was made. Into this, 110 tons of molten lead was poured to fabricate the *Ranger*'s keel.

Left: From the keel up, *Ranger*'s framework took shape in the big shed at Bath Iron Works, Bath, Maine. The *Ranger* is the first defender with an all-steel hull; her plates are thin, none greater than one-third of an inch thick.

Below: The *Ranger* has her decks cleared before launching. Her sleek hull is painted bronze, blue and white.

Above: Her mast lashed to her deck and her flags flying, the *Ranger* slid down into the water at a speed of 13½ knots going backward. Curious yachtsmen had a chance to note that she had an extraordinarily stubby bow, cut short to save weight.

Right: The $15,000, 165-foot duralumin mast, twelve stories tall, was stepped. While being towed through heavy seas to Newport, *Ranger* broke her mast. A costly duplicate was hastily rushed to completion.

Not all of this increased power is to be attributed, however, to form, much of it is due to improved methods of construction, by which the same strength of spars and hull is secured with the use of less material. In a yacht of a given displacement every pound of weight that can be taken out of the rigging, spars and hull may be placed in the lead keel with a consequent increase in sail-carrying power. Thus we find that the ballast (that is, the lead keel and the loose pig lead for trimming of the vessel) has gone up from 85 tons in Defender *to 90 tons in* Columbia, *and as high as 93 tons in* Constitution. Columbia *is a larger boat than* Defender *and probably is slightly heavier in construction; but as compared with* Columbia *the new boat, in spite of her greater beam and increased lead, will be of about the same displacement, a feat of construction of which the greatest credit is due to the designer.*

Radical Change in Construction

The considerable lightening of the hull of Constitution *(which be—if remembered, had been accompanied by a decided gain in strength) has been secured by a radical change in the method of framing. The usual system in yacht construction is to use shallow transverse frames, a few inches in depth, at intervals of 20 to 22 inches, throughout the whole length of the yacht. This is the system adopted in* Independence. *It is this framing that holds the hull to form, by resisting the transverse bending and crushing stresses; while the longitudinal stresses are taken up by the plating, assisted by two or four lines of stringers, as the case may be, by far the greater part of the longitudinal strains, however, falling upon the plating itself. Hence the latter must be made of greater weight than is actually necessary to enable it to act as the mere skin clothing of the frames. Herreshoff's innovation consists in running the framing of the yacht in both directions, using deep belt frames of an I-beam section for the transverse system of framing, and associating them with a system of longitudinal T-bar and angle-iron framing, which serves at once to take up a large proportion of longitudinal strains which ordinarily fall upon the plating, and so enables the weight of this plating to be very materially reduced. The transverse belt frames and the longitudinal framing are so arranged with regard to the width and lengths of the plating that the butt joints meet upon the frames, and the seams follow the longitudinal T-irons, thus doing away altogether with the weight of the washers and liners necessitated in riveting up a boat built in the conventional way.*

Judged from an engineering standpoint, this is a far more scientific distribution of the material to meet the special strains to which the hull of a yacht is subjected, particularly in a seaway. Just how great is the saving in weight is shown by the fact that although the superficial area of the Tobin bronze plating on Constitution *is greater than the superficial area of the bronze on* Independence, *the sheer strake in the latter being of steel, the total weight of the bronze plating actually laid on the Boston boat is a fraction under 30 tons, while the total weight of the plating in* Constitution *is slightly under 22 tons. Moreover, it must be remembered that this difference of 8 tons may be put into the keel without calling for a pound more of displacement, or the increase of a single square foot of wetted surface. This a clear gain due to good engineering; and surely the yacht designer who would dare to use 6/32-inch plating on the topsides of a 90-footer is entitled to all the gain in power and speed that are coming to him. Just here it may be well to state that no little of the credit of these successful results is due to that remarkable material Tobin bronze (the invention of a United States naval officer whose name it bears) which has come to be looked upon as an indispensable material for the plating of our American Cup defenders. Not only does it take on a wonderfully smooth polish, but it preserves it indefinitely; while it has the further invaluable quality of showing a tensile strength in the best specimens that is only a few pounds less than 40 tons to the square inch.*

In this period photo by J.C. Hemment, the *Defender*'s crew is handling her mainsail before her 1895 race with the *Valkyrie*.

Structural Details

The transverse belt frames, which are spaced 6 feet 8 inches apart, extend entirely around the hull and do duty at once as frames, floor plates, and deck beams. They are of I-beam section, the web from 5-40 to 4-40 of an inch thick and 15 inches deep amidships; the depth decreasing toward the ends, with flanges formed each of a pair of 1½ x 1½-inch angles. The belts are built up in sections, with a 2¼-inch lap at the joints riveted with a double row of ⅝ rivets. These beams, by virtue of their great depth, provide far greater stiffness than an equal weight of the shallow 4-inch bulb angles which are used in the conventional type of construction. Constitution *is not the first yacht to carry these frames, as they were used experimentally in last season's 70-footers. Mr. Herreshoff has profited by that experiment: for in a jump of a sea off Newport the frames buckled, the inner flanges springing out of line: hence the presence of diagonal braces of 1⅛-inch pipe which extend, in pairs, from the longitudinal T-irons to the inner flanges of the belts. These struts, moreover, afford stiffness in the longitudinal framing of hull and deck.*

The longitudinal framing consists of alternate 4½ x 4½-inch T-bars and 3 x 2 bulb angles, the T-bars follow the seams of the plating, which, in general, is 48-inches wide, and the angles are spaced midway between the T-bars. The belt frames are cut to allow those longitudinal frames to pass through, and the latter extend in unbroken lines from stem to stern, splice, the ends of the T-bars being joined with a U-iron splice, riveted to head and web of the bar, while the bulb angles are placed back to back, at the joints, and riveted. These longitudinal members are continuous and well riveted to the plating. It will be seen that they not merely keep the plating to shape, but also take a large share of the longitudinal stresses. Calculation of the weights of a given area of framing on Constitution *and* Independence *shows that there is not much weight saved in the framing alone, but it must be remembered that, weight for weight, it is a much stronger construction, the saving is in the weight of the plating, which Mr. Herreshoff has lightened out to the extent, as we have seen, of eight tons, as compared with* Independence. *Amidships there are seven strakes of plating. Commencing at the sheer strake, the thicknesses are 6-32, 6-32, 6-32, 7-32, 7-32, 7-32, and 8-32-inch. The first four strakes, to the top of the garboard strake, have flush seams; below this they are lap-joined. The sheer strake extends above the deck line and is riveted to a 2 x 2 bulbed angle, whose head forms the rail of the boat.*

THE FIN AND LEAD BULB

From station 28 to station 50 the belt-frames are carried down into the fin and riveted to the keel-plate, which is a Tobin bronze casting, ½-inch thick by 18-inches wide, with 4-inch side flanges, and transverse flanges at every frame station. At the three frame stations in the fin, intermediate between each belt-frame floor-plate, is an angle-iron frame. Of these, the center frame is a 1¾ x 1¾ plain angle, and the other two are 1 x 3 bulb angles. Here again Herreshoff has made a considerable saving in weight; for instead of running the floor plates down to the keel, the frames are tied together by a 12-inch keel plate, and a 12-inch floor-plate, with a 1¾-inch square tie-rod midway between them. These floor-plates commence at station 11 and extend aft to station 63. The framed structure of the fin terminates, as we have seen, in a half inch bronze keel plate, and below this plate the 95-ton belt of lead is hung in the following manner: First, the lowest strake of the bronze plating is extended down to overlap the lead by 20 inches, the latter being rabbeted [sic] *out to receive it. Through these plates 824 bronze tap-screws, $^5/_8$ x 6-inches, are screwed into the lead, 412 on each side. The keel is further supported by thirty-seven 1 x 10-inch vertical lag screws, which are screwed through the keel plate into the lead. If anyone cares to figure out the total section of the bronze bolts thus employed, he will find that there is an ample amount of holding strength, even should the* Constitution *experience a knockdown in a short, jumpy sea when the dynamic bending moment at the junction of the keel and lead might easily rise to the total of 400 or 500 foot-tons.*

THE MAST STEP

To provide the requisite strength of the mast-step (which, by the way, is placed 20-inches further aft than Columbia's *mast) an extra belt-frame is introduced, there being a belt-frame at the stations, 28, 30, and 32. The web of the frames is also increased to 7-40 of an inch. The step is formed by a combination of these frames with a deep keelson[5] of 7-16 inch steel worked intercostally between the frames, from station 24 to station 36, the keel plate being increased to $^5/_8$ of an inch in thickness beneath the mast, and for the full length of the mast-step. The keelson increases in depth from frame 24 to frame 28, where it reaches a maximum of 4 feet 6 inches, which depth it holds from frame 28 to frame*

32. From frame 32 it decreases in depth until it terminates at frame 36. The floor-plate portions of the frames 28, 30, and 32 carry the same depth as the keel plate. A $^5/_8$ inch, double, cover-plate closes in the mast-step, and below the cover-plate extends a deep, hollow, cone of $^5/_8$-inch plating which is riveted to the cover plate and the keelson. The upper flange of the cone consists of two 1½-inch angles, the outside diameter of the ring, formed by these flanges, being just 24 inches. The bottom of the steel mast will have riveted around it a 1½-inch angle-iron, with an outside diameter of 24 inches, and when the mast is in place it will be bolted down upon the cone by bolts which will pass through the ring on the mast and be made fast by nuts below the cone-ring. It is 6 feet 10 inches from the top of the step to the deck, and on each side of the mast-ring at the deck, intercostal plates are worked in between the belt-frames. The mast framing at the deck is stiffened against fore-and-aft racking strains by a trussing of hollow steel tubing, which extends in a fore-and-aft plane from the deck beams to the cover plate of the keelson. Three-inch tubular bilge struts extend from all the belt frames at the bilge to the same frames at the deck; but in the wake of the mast these struts are moved in to further assist in bracing the mast-ring and mast-step construction. The whole design is entirely novel, and shows the characteristic resourcefulness of the Bristol designer. It is extremely stiff and strong and gives evidence that Herreshoff has learned the lesson of the buckled mast-steps with which he was troubled in previous defenders. In one of these, a step which had a calculated resistance to crushing of 250 tons showed signs of buckling when the yacht was being sailed hard in the scend[6] of a heavy sea. The deck is carried by the belt frames and by longitudinal lines of 1 $^5/_8$ bulb angles, which later extend in unbroken lines from stem to stern, passing through apertures cut for them in the belt-frames. Galvanized steel deck plating is used, and to protect it from the weather, it is covered with a preparation of cork tiling which is impervious to water and at the same time adds but very slightly to the weight of the deck.

SAIL PLAN

From what has been said about lowering of weights in Constitution and the increased power of her form, it is evident that she can swing aloft a spread of sail which will rival that of the Independence in area. Compared with Columbia, the boom will be lengthened to 1,110 feet, *about 4 feet will be added to the hoist, the fore triangle will be lengthened, as will the topmast and gaff, with the result that a total of 14,400 square feet of sail will be carried—an area which may be subsequently decreased or added to according to the ability of the boat as shown in her tuning up. All things considered, we look for* Constitution *to beat* Columbia *over a thirty-knot course by not less than ten minutes in light airs and five minutes in a breeze. This would mean an advantage of respectively eighteen minutes and eleven minutes over* Shamrock I *under the form which the latter yacht showed over here.*

Chapter 7
Meeting the Challengers
(1870–1887)

Following the race of 1851, yachting in America went quietly along. After the American Civil War came the era of the big schooners. The memorable ocean race in December 1866 between the American schooners the *Henrietta*, the *Fleetwing* and the *Vesta*, with other visits of the *Sappho* and the *Dauntless* to the waters of the British Isles, together with notable improvements in the English fleet since the visit of the *America*, finally lead to the first challenge for the Cup.

James Ashbury was the first challenger for the America's Cup, and that unforgettable race was in 1870. Ashbury represented the Royal Thames Yacht Club, the *Cambria*'s owner of record. Though the *Cambria* was not the fastest of her class, she was unwavering, sturdy and a comfortably reliable seagoing vessel. She was a keel craft of good model, noticeably different from the antiquated models that the *America* had whipped twenty years earlier.

Ashbury was given a taste of the medicine the English had given the *America*. He was forced to race his *Cambria* against a fleet of twenty-three American schooners, each skipper more interested in beating the British than winning the race for himself. Nine Americans, led by the *Magic*, finished ahead of the *Cambria*. Ill fate befell the *Cambria* when she lost her port shroud and fore topmast-backstay when she was struck by another boat. Fourth to cross the line was the *America*, still fast after nineteen years, though she had gone through the Civil War as a Confederate blockade runner and a Union gunboat.

Against this armada, the *Cambria* could hardly be expected to win. The New York Yacht Club, holders of the Cup, was severely criticized after this match.

Mr. Ashbury continued a tirade of protests, but undaunted, he brought his yacht the *Livonia* to challenge again in 1871. The *Livonia* was built, for the specific purpose of competing for the Cup, by Michael Ratsey, of Cowes, for Ashbury. Although intended expressly for racing in American waters, she was of the same general type, but an improved *Cambria* model, a sturdy keel schooner of the prevailing heavy wooden type.

This series was preceded by much unpleasant correspondence before an understanding was reached as to terms. Ashbury wished to represent twelve British yacht clubs at one time so that if he lost the first time he would have eleven more chances.

Because of the protests by Ashbury and some influential members of the New York Yacht Club, some great changes of opinion as to the method of defending the Cup came about. It was decided to sail a series of races instead of a single race and to put one yacht, not the entire fleet, against the challenger. However, the Club declined to select one yacht alone as defender for the entire series but instead asserted the right to select a defender for each race.

The challenger was met by four defenders ready to do battle. The *Columbia* won the first two races but was disabled in the third, giving the win to the *Livonia*. For the fourth race, the *Sappho* was substituted for the *Columbia*, which won the next two races, and the Americans declared that the match was over, having won four out of a possible seven.

Ashbury protested again and threatened legal action. This was an unfortunate beginning for what was intended for the world stage to display the lofty ideals of good sportsmanship. However, Ashbury's protests had some effect, because never again was a challenger forced to meet more than one defending yacht.

In 1876, the third challenge came unexpectedly from the Royal Canadian Yacht Club based in Toronto. Canada's first challenge, with a Great Lakes schooner, the *Countess of Dufferin*, was a yacht modeled and built by Alexander Cuthbert, a Canadian of considerable ability but whose experience was wholly in yachts of the ordinary American type. The new challenger was built by a syndicate of Canadian yachtsmen who, without the necessary capital for such an enterprise, sponsored a yacht very much inferior in construction, finish and rig.

The yacht chosen as the single defender to meet the Canadian was the *Madeleine*. She was one of the fastest of the centerboard type; she was from the mind and yard of James E. Smith of Nyack. The *Madeleine*, originally a sloop, like the *Magic*, but enlarged and altered (ninety-five feet waterline, twenty-four feet abeam and seven feet draft) from time to time, became almost a new yacht.

The challenging boat was badly beaten in two races by the *Madeleine*. This was the last series sailed in schooners.

It is interesting to note that the *America*, now twenty-five years old, followed the contestants around the course in the second race, proving herself to be a better boat than the Canadian.

Prior to the 1881 challenge, in 1879, a new Yankee centerboard sloop called the *Mischief* was launched; she was a modified yacht in accordance with new theories of the racing model: plumb stern, straight sheer and higher free-board, with a shapely, though short, overhang suggesting the hull of a cutter. She was rather wide, nearly twenty feet on sixty-one feet waterline, and she drew nearly six feet. At the time, she was a marked departure from the older boats of her class, especially because she was an iron-hulled vessel; consequently, she carried her ballast, all lead, at a very low point.

The first trial races ever held for selection of the Cup defender took place in October 1881; the *Mischief* was awarded the extreme honor to defend the Cup. After the trials, the *Mischief* was hauled out, her iron bottom scraped and sandpapered, carefully painted with red lead and covered with multiple coats of varnish into which "pot-lead," or graphite, was rubbed with brushes until the entire hull shone like a mirror. Above deck, the *Mischief* was superior in rigging and canvas, and she came to the starting line on November 9 for the first race in faultless racing trim.

This second attempt by the Canadians to wrench the Cup from the New York Yacht Club was by entering the sloop *Atalanta* as the challenger. She was attached to the Bay of Quinte Yacht Club of Belleville, Canada, and for the first time in the history of the Cup, the challenge was from a single-stick vessel: a centerboard sloop of the American type, sixty-four feet waterline, nineteen feet beam and five feet, six inches draft. Again, unfortunately, her owners had underestimated the cost to finish and rig the craft; she suffered from inferior finish, sails and gear.

The *Atalanta*'s launching was late, so in order to save time she was brought to New York via the Erie Canal, which was a feat of some magnitude. The yacht's beam was too broad to pass through the canal's narrow locks. She eventually squeezed through by shifting her ballast, which listed her to one side, and by securing her mast and spars on deck. Unfortunately, the Canadian challenger, though of good model, was lacking in everything that makes a good racing yacht: her wooden bottom was rough in spite of planing and painting in the New York yard, her rig and equipment were poor, her sails poorly cut and she was badly manned and handled. Adding to her problems, the Canadians arrived in New York on October 30, several weeks after the end of the normal racing season. Sadly, our friendly neighbors suffered an inglorious defeat in two races against the *Mischief.*

After the first four matches for the America's Cup, little of consequence advanced in American yacht designs. The first three races were sailed by schooners, in which American boats have always outclassed their British cousins, while the fourth was sailed by the Canadian-built sloop the *Countess of Dufferin.* The first step of true development came with departure from the accepted model, and that was induced by the challenge of the *Genesta* in December 1884.

Early in 1885, leading members of the Eastern Yacht Club, Vice-Commodore H. Malcolm Forbes, General Charles J. Paine and Secretary Edward Burgess met in Boston and began planning a boat for the defense of the Cup. Their plan embodied using the most advanced and scientific ideas extant about the building of a speedy racing yacht.

About the same time, Commodore Bennett and Vice-Commodore William P. Douglas of the New York Yacht Club commissioned Mr. A. Cory Smith of New York to build a sloop for the same purpose. The product of the New York syndicate was the *Priscilla,* an enlarged *Mischief,* while that of the Boston group was the *Puritan*—a radical departure from all previous types.

The *Puritan* was principally the product of the scientific ideas of young Boston naval architect Edward Burgess. Burgess had designed some fast cats and other small boats, but the *Puritan* would be his first major contract outside of the Hub. In three major aspects, the *Puritan* was a departure from all previously accepted types. Usually, the relation of beam to length had been one to three, but in the *Puritan* that number was reduced to one to four. There was a slight increase of actual draft, though the relation of draft to waterline length was somewhat less than that of the *Gracie.* The latter—with a waterline of 69 feet 3½ inches—drew 8 feet, while the former—with 81.1 feet waterline—drew only 8 feet 10 inches. The secret was in the disposition of the ballast, for this was how the *Puritan* differed most radically from any sloop that had been built on typical American lines before her.

Puritan's ballast was a strip of lead forty-five feet long, two feet wide and sixteen inches thick. Weighing forty-eight tons, it was bolted on the outside of her keel. Besides that, she had an iron shoe weighing nine hundred pounds on the foot of her centerboard. The *Gracie, Fanny* and other racing sloops carried pig iron between their ribs for ballast, but in this instance, besides a great increase of ballast, there was a concentration of it below the keel, the

The 1886 challenger, the *Galatea*.

result of which was an important gain in stability. The idea of placing the ballast below the keel was borrowed from the English, who had long used it.

The *Puritan*, with her straight stem, high bow and long overhang astern, differed so widely in appearance from her predecessors that, in the eyes of

New York yachtsmen, she did not present the appealing figure of the typical racing vessel. She was considered by Captain Roland F. Coffin, the most competent yacht reporter of the time, to have the look "of an old North River sloop." Yet by late twentieth-century standards, she was viewed as a really handsome and powerful vessel.

The type of yacht to which the peculiarities of the English coast had given rise was further modified by the rules of the English Yacht Racing Association. Thus, the typical English cutter, of which the *Genesta* was a fair representative, became a long, narrow, deep vessel, non-capsizable but prone to lie down and sail on her side, and with a lack of buoyancy that made her ride through the waves rather than over them.

The supremacy of the *Puritan* under all conditions, and on all points of sailing except running, was conclusively demonstrated in the match. Several abortive attempts to sail the first race confirmed her ability to beat the English boat easily in light weather. In the first completed race over the regular New York Yacht Club course, from Owl's Head to the entrance to the Narrows, in a breeze light at the beginning but stiff over three-quarters of the course, she beat the *Genesta* by the decisive margin of sixteen minutes, nineteen seconds, corrected time.

The second race over an ocean course from the Scotland Lightship—twenty miles to leeward and return, sailed in a strong breeze from the start and a gale toward the close—was not won so easily, but better handling, rather than parity in the qualities of the yachts, accounted for the fine showing of the Englishmen. The *Puritan* finished two minutes ahead and won by one minute, thirty-eight seconds, corrected time.

The result of the *Puritan-Genesta* match initiated a departure in English yacht design, but this was not made apparent in the succeeding match of 1886 because the challenge of the *Galatea* had been issued at the same time as that of the *Genesta*. Because of the *Galatea*'s poor showing in the few races she entered during the season, she did not come up to the *Genesta*'s standard, and the feeling was that she would make a poor showing against the *Puritan*. Therefore, there was no urgent need to build a new defender, but General Charles J. Paine thought differently. The outcome of Paine's decision was the contract given to Edward Burgess to design the *Mayflower*. In several important respects, the *Mayflower* differed from the *Puritan*. She had greater waterline length, less proportional beam, more draft, more ballast and a larger sail area.

The *Galatea* did not differ greatly from the *Genesta* except in size. Although a longer and leaner vessel, her lines were not as fine. In comparison, the *Genesta* differed in size from the *Mayflower*; she was longer, deeper, more heavily ballasted and had $8^{1}/_{2}$ feet fewer beam and 1,129 square feet fewer sail area. Because of her inferiority in beam and sail area, she was given a time allowance from the *Mayflower*, which was fully able to give—as the result of the races proved.

Soon after the *Mayflower*'s victory, the New York Yacht Club received notice from the Royal Clyde Yacht Club of a challenge for the succeeding year; for the first time since 1871, England was building a yacht for the specific purpose of capturing the Cup.

This vessel, the *Thistle*, was a radical departure from the cutter type. Here, it is interesting to note that as the Americans had abandoned some American ideas and favored some English ideas, so the English abandoned some of their old ideas and leaned toward American models. This nod to certain aspects of the other's ideas was not an expression of copying ideas; rather, it was a rational advance toward a new common type.

While the Americans realized the importance of beam and the value of draft, the English, who had almost whittled draft out of existence, were forced to admit its effectiveness as a factor of speed. The result of this change in thought amounted to the *Thistle*. With a bit more than 1 foot less length on the waterline than *Galatea*, she had over one-third more beam. Another important result amounted to ten tons fewer ballast and a bit more than three inches in draft, and thus she was able to carry 1,463 square feet more sail.

As soon as the dimensions of the steel-hulled *Thistle* were received at the New York Yacht Club, General Paine and designer Edward Burgess began construction of a new sloop intended to be an improvement upon the *Mayflower*.[7] Because it afforded the maximum strength with the minimum weight, steel was the construction material Burgess chose for the *Volunteer*.

Along the steps previously noted in the development of Cup defenders, there was a great tendency to shorten the yacht's underbody relatively to the rest of the construction. The *Puritan* was 12 feet, $10^{1}/_{2}$ inches longer overall than on the waterline. The *Mayflower* was 14 feet, 5 inches longer than the *Puritan*. This tendency, the object of which was to decrease friction and increase speed in reaching and running, was carried still further in the *Volunteer*, which was 20.35 feet longer overall than on the waterline.

The *Volunteer* was only about $^{3}/_{10}$ of a foot shorter on the waterline than the *Mayflower* and about $^{4}/_{10}$ of a foot less beam but exactly the same draft, with five tons more ballast.

It is reported that the *Volunteer* presented her owners none of the disappointments incident to a new boat built exclusively for racing. Not even

The 1886 defender, the sloop *Mayflower*, was designed by Edward Burgess for General Charles J. Paine.

Lord Dunraven's cutter *Valkyrie* was a mighty sailor, but she could not outsail Herreshoff's *Vigilant*.

the *Mayflower* could approach her in speed on their first encounter; she won every race she entered during the selection races. Without hesitation, she was selected to meet the *Thistle*.

We have read that the *Thistle* was by far the most handsome and fastest boat that had yet come over seeking the Cup, but she was not fast enough. The *Volunteer* showed her superiority at the very outset of the first race, which she won, over the club course, by 19 minutes 23¾ seconds, after allowing the *Thistle* 5 seconds.

The second race, sailed over a forty-mile ocean course with a beat to windward at the start and a run home in a stiff breeze, was not such a cakewalk for the *Volunteer*, but she won by the decisive corrected time of 11 minutes 48¾ seconds. And so the 1887 challenge, the seventh unsuccessful attempt to wrest the America's Cup from the halls of the New York Yacht Club, is a matter for marine historians to ponder.

Until 1893, all matches had included one race in Lower New York Bay; the others sailed in the ocean off Sandy Hook. From 1893 until 1903, all matches were sailed off Sandy Hook, except for the first race in 1895, which was held off Seabright, New Jersey. The 1920 series was sailed off Ambrose Light Vessel, and all subsequent matches were held in Rhode Island Sound off Newport, Rhode Island. The races' locations changed when, in 1980, the *Freedom* lost the Cup to the *Australia*.

John Brown Herreshoff had such an exquisite and singular genius for fine shipbuilding that his blindness was no impediment. He studied all the company's matters out in his head and kept countless details of all the vessels he had ever built in his extraordinary brain. Often he would be guided up to a vessel on which work was being done, and by putting a hand on the hull, he would give it its name. That twinkle of humor amused J.B. and his visitors, but it was the record of Cup defenders he and his brother designed and built that brought them prestigious customers from 1893 to 1914.

Chapter 8
The Herreshoff Defenders
(1893-1937)

Early in the 1870s, when the shoal centerboard sloop and the schooner were being developed and perfected, there arose in Bristol, Rhode Island, the Herreshoff Manufacturing Company, which was noted for many speedy yachts, both open catboats and larger-decked craft. By the mid-1870s the Herreshoff yard had turned its attention from sailing craft to steam yachts. So engrossed were they in their new enterprise that they altogether abandoned their attention on the debate surrounding the *Puritan-Genesta* and the Cup races. At the same time, the sailing instincts of Nathanael Herreshoff kept him with a keel cruiser anchored off his waterfront home on Bristol Harbor.

Seasoned yachtsmen frequently discussed the abilities of the Herreshoffs as design rivals of Ed Burgess. Around the turn of the twentieth century, many a worried yachtsman came to the Bristol, Rhode Island shipyard of the Herreshoff Manufacturing Co. for racing sloops to beat off the British challengers for the America's Cup—and they came to the right place.

Before the next challenge was received, a new figure in yacht designing had come aboard, and a new type of boat had come onto the scene. At the peak of his career, Ed Burgess died; but the genius of yacht designing had not passed with him. Another hand, even more cunning, took up the pencil where he had put it down, and that hand developed novel and winning vessels. In the summer of 1891, an odd-looking sloop made her debut in New York waters. Though only forty-six feet on the waterline, she was seventy feet overall. Yachtsmen at first laughed at her long, pig-shaped nose and flaring convex bows, but then they marveled at her sailing qualities.

Here we are afforded a fine view of the *Gloriana*'s innovative keel.

Nothing in her class could keep within sight of her. She fairly reveled in rough weather and could go outside of Sandy Hook and sail a race in a seaway that would stagger a yacht twice her size; she rode the waves like a duck. This was the *Gloriana*, built for E.D. Morgan of New York by the Herreshoff Manufacturing Co. of Bristol, Rhode Island.

The boat building firm's partners were John Brown Herreshoff, known as "the blind boat builder of Bristol," and his young scientific-minded brother, Nathanael Greene Herreshoff, known as the Wizard of Bristol but addressed as Captain Nat. Captain Nat's inspiration for the *Gloriana* was a light draft craft used for generations by sports fishermen in Barnegat Bay. He took this as the type for his upper body and added stability by devising a deep, thin under body, heavily weighted at the foot; the result worked a revolution in yachting.

The *Vigilant* during her shakedown in Bristol, Rhode Island Harbor. *A photo by C.E. Bolles published in* Munsey's Magazine, *September 1893.*

THE *VIGILANT*, 1893

The challenge of the *Valkyrie II* in 1893 brought out three new boats to try out for the privilege of defending the Cup. They were the *Vigilant*, the *Colonia* and the *Pilgrim*. The first two were built by the Herreshoffs and the last by a Boston firm. The *Vigilant* was a centerboard, the *Colonia* a keel craft;

the struggle to be declared the defender was confined to these two, which had the same upper-body type as the *Gloriana*. The Boston boat could not keep pace with the Bristol boats. The *Volunteer*, which had been changed to a schooner and re-rigged as a sloop to act as a "trial horse," made a poor showing alongside Captain Nat's creations.

The *Vigilant*, built of Tobin bronze for strength and lightness, showed to be the better all-around boat and was selected as the defender of the Cup. The *Viligant*'s principal dimensions were overall length, 126 feet; waterline, 86.2; beam, 26; draft, 13.3; and sail area, 11,272 square feet.

The *Valkyrie II*, like the *Thistle*, was designed by George L. Watson, one of England's foremost yacht designers, with especial view to meeting the conditions of American waters. She was an advancement of the *Thistle* model—in other words, a wider departure from the old English cutter type—while the appearance of her bow indicated that the good points of the *Gloriana* had not been entirely overlooked by her designer. She was only nine inches shorter on the waterline than the *Vigilant*, and she carried 1,230 square feet less sail.

As in all previous matches, the superiority was on the side of the defender. Three races were sailed, and the *Vigilant* easily won the first and second, by five minutes, forty-eight seconds and ten minutes, thirty-five seconds, respectively, after allowing the *Valkyrie II* one minute, forty-eight seconds. The third race was also won, but by the narrow margin of forty seconds.

THE *DEFENDER*, 1893

When Lord Dunraven issued another challenge for 1895, New York Yacht Club members C.O. Iselin, William K. Vanderbilt and E.D. Morgan, who had been members of the syndicate that built the *Vigilant*, commissioned the Herreshoffs to build them a new boat, to be called *Defender*.

The following narrative describing the *Defender*'s attributes is taken from the September 1895 issue of *Munsey's Magazine* by an anonymous author:

> *Like a great white cloud coming on the wind, or some wonderful bird from the regions of snow,* Defender *sailed down the sound from her cradle at Bristol, proud, graceful, and confident. It was the confidence of her superiority she seemed to show, a confidence in the magic of her lines and the might of her white sails, a proud certainty that she could out sail all that had gone before her, and, above all, a pride in the knowledge that upon*

The *Defender*. Munsey's Magazine, *September 1895*.

her depended the honor of American yachting, that made Defender *seem all but human, and impressed those who beheld her with the feeling that she was built to win.*

Designed and constructed by the Herreshoffs, a firm of American yacht builders famous for the records their boats have always made, under the personal supervision of men whose yachting experience in the defense of the Cup had made them familiar with the defects of the past, and on the order of a syndicate which set no money limit, Defender *has come to her task the perfect embodiment of all that experience, thought, and money can make a boat—as perfect a racing machine as ever left her cradle.*

Yachting today comes so near flying that the development of the sport may, after all, be the initiative step in the art of navigating the air. It is this theory that the Herreshoffs had in mind when they designed Defender. *The idea was to get the least resistance and give the greatest power, to hold as little as possible to the water and take as much as possible to the air. For a boat of her size* Defender *resists the water less than any craft afloat. The chief characteristic of the American boat, heretofore, the centerboard, has been abandoned that the hull might have its weight on its keel—which the fin prevented. Above the keel the task has been to secure buoyancy; but at the edge of the water the art of yacht building seems to have given place to that of flying. Thousands of feet of canvas stretch up and out into the air like monster wings, the question* Defender *answers is: what is the greatest amount of canvas a boat can stand and yet keep the necessary running grip on the water? So skillfully has this problem been handled, that the whole yachting world is marveling at the expanse of canvas the yacht is able to spread—between twelve and thirteen thousand square feet.*

Since Defender*'s first trials it has been evident to her sailing masters, the only ones at all fit to judge, that in light winds she was a much faster boat than the last defender of the Cup,* Vigilant. *Her general work has not been altogether satisfactory to those who know of her powers only through what they read. She was expected to sail away from* Vigilant *easily, and she defeated the [Jay] Gould boat with but a narrow margin. It is the light wind; however that she will probably have to sail under in the race, and a light wind boat that she will have to meet.*

In the *Defender*, the Herreshoffs developed the fin keel. She was constructed of aluminum and bronze, 2 feet shorter than the *Vigilant* overall but $2 \, ^3/_{10}$ feet longer on the waterline, had about 3 feet less beam and 6 feet more draft. During trials against the *Vigilant*, she showed from the beginning superiority on every point of sailing and was chosen to meet the British newcomer, *Valkyrie III*.

The *Valkyrie III*, like her predecessors in the last two matches, had been designed by Watson. She was a much larger and more powerful vessel than her namesake in the 1893 race, and her sail area was even greater than that of the *Defender*. Thus, the two nations had very nearly reached the common type to which they had for almost a decade been approaching.

Returning to the September 1895 issue of *Munsey's Magazine* narrative, this is what the contemporary author thought of the Valkyrie III:

> *Lord Dunraven, in making a final attempt to recover the Queen's* [America's] *Cup, has endeavored, in* Valkyrie III, *to show how much he has learned from the defeat he suffered at the hand of* Vigilant *two years ago. In design and build his boat has had of English skill and general experience all that* Defender *claimed from America. Mr.* [George L.] *Watson, her maker, sailed with* Valkyrie II *when she raced* Vigilant, *and knew what was wanted, and what was expected of the new boat. For light winds, he has undoubtedly produced the fastest boat ever built in England.* Valkyrie III *showed this clearly in the run of June 29 with* Britannia *and* Ailsa *at Rothesay, and again on the 15ᵗʰ of July in a run and reach of thirteen miles, in which she came in ten minutes ahead of the same competitors.*
>
> *After his defeat here in 1893, Dunraven made the remark that* Valkyrie *was no drifter, the accepted lesson of that defeat explains the character of the new challenger, and clears the mystery of her wonderful sailing in light winds. Certain it was that after the third race with* Vigilant *the English lord had the drifting speed of a boat well in mind, and in his molding of another* Valkyrie *challenger Watson doubtless gave the matter serious thought. Experts assert that it is this that gives* Valkyrie III *her great grace and beauty; but they express fear that she may be too tender a craft to stand up to her task of carrying her sails in a strong wind.*
>
> *Yachting men on the Clyde seem to place no great amount of confidence in* Valkyrie III. *The most they say is that she has a fair chance. Some condemn her wholly because she shows a few lines that are unmistakably American.*
>
> *A glimpse of the models of the two racers reveals in each a singular imitation on the part of the designers—a delicate exchange of compliments, perhaps.* Herreshoff *has imitated the* Valkyrie II; Watson *has taken many of the lines of* Vigilant. *In the last Cup race both of these yacht makers saw good points in the rival boat, and each builder took advantage of what he saw.*

The best that has been said of Valkyrie III *was the expression made by Mr. Watson, when he remarked, "She satisfies me."*

The essential differences between the two boats are shown by the following figures. Those of the *Defender*: overall length, 124 feet; waterline, 88.5; beam, 23.3; draft, 19; and sail area, 12,650 square feet. The *Valkyrie III*: overall length, 125; waterline, 88.85; beam, 23; draft, 16; and sail area, 13,028 square feet.

When the boats were measured,[8] it was found that, for the first time in the struggles between "single-stickers," time allowance had to be given by the challenger to the defender. As thirty-mile races had been decided on, the *Valkyrie III* allowed twenty-nine seconds. The first race, sailed in a light breeze over a moderate groundswell, showed the superiority, both on and off the wind, of the *Defender*, which won by the comfortable margin of eight minutes, forty-nine seconds, corrected time. In the second encounter the *Defender*, although crippled immediately before the start by a deliberate foul and thereby compelled to carry less canvas than her adversary, sailed a magnificent race, actually beating the *Valkyrie III* over two-thirds of the course and finishing only one minute, sixteen seconds behind—on corrected time, forty-seven seconds. *Defender*'s owner, Mr. C. Oliver Iselin, protested the foul, and the committee gave the win to the *Defender*, which the circumstances warranted.

Lord Dunraven then withdrew from the match and sailed home in a huff.

THE *COLUMBIA*, 1899 AND 1901

It is always interesting to read contemporary period publications' observations of notable events recorded soon after their occurrence. Here is the description of the launching of the *Columbia* from the *American Monthly Review of Reviews*, July 1899.

At a quarter past 8 on the evening of June 10, Mrs. C. Oliver Iselin broke a bottle of champagne over the prow of the new Cup defender in the Herreshoff yards at Bristol. "I christen thee Columbia *and I wish thee luck," said she.*

Simultaneous with the crash of shattered glass the beautiful bronze, with her under body gleaming like gold and her top sails glistening white, began to move slowly toward the water as the gigantic windlass attached to the steel cradle on which she was built revolved.

In this trial race off Larchmont, Long Island, the *Defender* and the *Columbia* are jockeying for the start. The *Columbia* got well to windward before the start, so she was able to run down and cross the line one second ahead. The stake-boat is just off the *Defender*'s bow.

With the first sign of motion came lusty cheers from 5,000 throats, ear-piercing shrieks from strident whistles, and salutes from yacht cannon. The scene was spectacular. It was rendered more theatric still because of the powerful calcium lights flashed on the shapely hull from the tender St. Michael.

As the Columbia *emerged from the shed Capt. Charles Barr, who with Nat Herreshoff and half a dozen sailors was on her deck, erected a flag-staff and broke out an immense silken yacht ensign. A few moments later the private signals of her owners, Commodore Morgan and Mr. Iselin, were displayed from a jury-mast stepped in the aperture for the immense spar of Oregon pine which is to be placed in position immediately. The darkness of the night was made brilliant by the flash-lights of photographers and the glare of search-lights, all aimed at the hull of white and gold moving with grace and dignity to its baptism of seawater. Seventeen minutes elapsed before the stately fabric floated clear of the cradle and danced buoyantly in the element she is destined to adorn.*

A yachtsman of even ten years ago [1888] *who had not kept up with the course of events in the '90s would not be a little astonished at the* Columbia. *She is of the fin-keel type (that queer modern shape whose name is very descriptive and which gives her, with a beam of 24 feet, no less than 20 feet draught), and to the uninitiated she is hardly to be distinguished from* Defender. *The experts pick her out by minute differences in spreaders, counter, nose and gaff topsail, quite invisible to an untrained eye. In reality she exhibits the other boat's characteristic features in an even more marked degree, having a still longer overhang forward and aft (the particular improvement introduced by the Herreshoffs), a greater cutting away of the fore-foot, still more rake in the stern-post, a flatter floor, deeper draught, smaller wetted surface, and more sail area.*

A few figures will give an idea of what a peculiar racing machine had been evolved by modern competition. With a total length of 131 feet, Columbia*'s load water-line measures only 89 feet 6 inches; that is to say, one-third of her length is "in the air" as receding bow and overhanging stern. Her "backbone" is an inch thick bronze keel-plate, reinforced by three inches of flanges and cross-webs, so that there is in effect four inches of metal to carry, below, the great lead keel weighing 90 tons; above, the floors and frames of the vessel. The huge stick of Oregon pine first used as a mast was 107½ feet long and weighed about 4 tons. At this writing [1899] it is being replaced by a steel mast a few inches shorter and tapering both ways from a center diameter of 22¼ inches. This will take off fully a ton of weight above the deck and is expected to make the boat much stiffer in the wind. Her topmast is 68 feet long, bowsprit 38, spinnaker 73, and she can carry sails aggregating 13,500 square feet—nearly 1,000 more than* Defender.

The author of this article goes on with several more interesting facts. The professional American crew of thirty-four sailors, four quartermasters and a second mate, all hailed from Deer Island, Maine, and they were managed by owner C. Oswald Iselin and sailing master Scotsman Charlie Barr, who had sailed the *Minerva* and the *Colonia* to victory in nearly every race that they were entered. The crew earned $45 a month and an additional $4 for each race. It is assumed that the crew was promised a healthy-sized bonus if the *Columbia* successfully defended the Cup. It is further assumed that the wealthy gentlemen who supplied this defender probably shelled out well over $250,000 toward the effort.

The *Columbia*, Nat Herreshoff's masterpiece of beauty and speed, successful defender of the Cup in the 1899 match, was selected once again to meet the challenger in the 1901 match. Although this would seem to be a precedent-setting decision, it was the only time that the same yacht defended

The sloop *Independence* at her 1901 coming out.

the Cup in two consecutive races until 1967 and 1970, when the *Intrepid* was the defender, and 1974 and 1977, when the *Courageous* defended the Cup. Both of these yachts were the designs of Olin J. Stephens.

The run-up to the selection of the *Columbia* as defender consisted of match races between Herreshoff-built *Columbia* and *Constitution* and Boston-built *Independence*.

The *Independence* was designed by B.B. Crowninshield, who belonged to a family long involved in Salem shipping. Popular thought in Boston was that the new yacht could easily beat all the New York boats as General Paine had with the *Puritan*, *Mayflower* and *Volunteer*. As it turned out, the designer had all the troubles that could be imagined because the hull, spars, rigging, fittings and sails were all built by separate companies and came together as pieces in a jigsaw puzzle.

In his 1963 book, *An Introduction to Yachting*, L. Francis Herreshoff relates his personal observation of the *Independence*: "I must say that when I saw the picture of the *Independence* I thought my father's cup boats would be beaten by *Independence*, but things turned out quite differently for she had structural trouble and leaked badly; she did not steer well, and her very flat model had so much wetted surface that she was very dull in light weather."

The other new Cup boat for 1901 was *Constitution*, built for a syndicate of New York Yacht Club members headed by August Belmont. She was designed by Captain Nat and managed by William Butler Duncan, who had run *Defender* when she was the trial boat for *Columbia* in 1899. In model and sail plan, *Constitution* was an enlarged *Columbia*, but her construction was quite novel, for she was the first vessel built on what is called longitudinal framing over widely spaced web frames, a construction that has the advantages of:

- greater strength for its weight
- plating can be laid flush with one of the longitudinal frames making a continuous butt strap at the seams
- local strains, such as the mast step, et cetera, can be taken care of by the location of the web frames
- this type of framing, when properly designed, is the cheapest

The *Columbia*'s owners, J. Pierpont Morgan and Edwin D. Morgan, had their 1899 Cup defender refitted and enlisted Skipper Charlie Barr to return to the helm of the boat that he had steered to victory against the *Shamrock* two years earlier.

During the trial races, observers were surprised by the strong performance of *Columbia*. A sportswriter for the *New York Tribune* wrote of the July 2, 1901 race: "Barr was crouching over his wheel and sailing *Columbia* fine, some said too fine, but Barr knows his boat and he was now steering for his future and his reputation."

It is important to add that he was in perfect symbiosis with his Scandinavian crew. The sail trim was always perfect, the spinnaker was hoisted in less time than the others and the boat slipped around the marks "as if she were a catboat!"

Fascinated by Charlie Barr's talent, the famous American historian W.P. Stephens wrote that the ex-Scotsman "handled *Columbia* as a man would a bicycle." Certainly, he had the slower sailboat, but he made life hard for Rhodes, and as Thomas F. Day observed, "Barr simply made a monkey of the other man…forcing him to do whatever he wished."

According to L. Francis Herreshoff, *Columbia* and *Constitution* met twenty times during that summer. Each yacht won nine of the meets, and two races were called off for lack of wind. Later in that season of trials, *Columbia* won regularly. Because the two yachts were so evenly matched, the win went to whoever got the start. The Cup Committee chose the *Columbia* to meet the *Shamrock II*.

During the 1901 struggle, the *Shamrock II* is leading the *Columbia*. This image is from a glass magic lantern slide.

This is an enlargement of the *Columbia* from a magic lantern slide.

Early on the morning of October 4, the day of the third and final race, Captain Barr and sailmaker Mr. Hathaway from the Herreshoff sail loft attempted to shorten the head rope of the *Columbia*'s mainsail. *Columbia*'s sails were old and had stretched out considerably, and the head of the mainsail was now longer than the gaff.

The *Columbia* beat the *Shamrock II* in all three meets. The first race on September 28 was a thirty-mile windward-leeward course that *Columbia* won by one minute, twenty seconds, corrected time. The second race took place on October 3 on a thirty-mile triangular course; *Columbia* beat *Shamrock II* by three minutes, forty-five seconds, corrected time. The third race took place on October 4 over a forty-mile windward-leeward course that the *Columbia* won by forty-one seconds corrected time; actually, the *Shamrock II* had beaten *Columbia* by two seconds, elapsed time.

THE *RELIANCE*, 1903

The *Reliance*, reputed to be the largest and fastest Cup defender ever built, was certainly a masterpiece and the thoroughbred of the genre.

Herreshoff's magnificent racing machine, the *Reliance*. The *Reliance* is the image on the U.S. quarter dollar coin honoring the state of Rhode Island. *Period postcard.*

Masterminding the New York Yacht Club's effort to retain the Cup was the scientific-minded Captain Nat, an innovative designer and engineer who had created three previous Cup defenders—each different than the other. When the *Reliance* emerged from the Herreshoff Manufacturing Co.'s shed into Bristol Harbor, in the words of the report of the local newspaper, "Loud and boisterous cheers filled the air." The *Reliance* was, in the minds of seasoned yachtsmen, a "skimming dish," a flat-bottomed, shallow-draft hull modeled on inland racing scows, of course including a few key Herreshoff modifications for sailing in rough weather.

Under the measurement rule governing the series, only the waterline length and sail area were computed to gauge the yacht's handicap. The two designers built yachts that were 90 feet on the waterline; both were longer if the bow and stern overhangs were counted. Each contender carried an enormous amount of sail; the *Shamrock III* carried 14,154 square feet, and the *Reliance* carried 16,159 square feet. For the *Reliance*, it was the largest sail plan ever set on a single-masted yacht; but in other elements of their designs, nearly opposite ideas prevailed. Fife, the challenger's designer, took a more traditional and conservative course, while Herreshoff's design was radical and experimental.

The *Bristol Phoenix* reporter continued:

> *While the final trials for the honor of defending the cup will not begin until July thirtieth, it seems almost certain that the* Reliance *will be chosen. She has shown up superbly in almost every sort of sea, in light and strong winds alike. She has beaten by over twenty minutes the record for a windward and leeward course of thirty miles. Granted her superiority to* Constitution *and* Columbia, *it is, however, safe to say that this superiority is not as great as the recent race figures seem to show. She is better canvassed than the* Constitution, *and is managed by Captain Barr, while* Columbia *is sailed by an amateur—which makes a lot of difference. The* Reliance *is built, to a considerable extent, along the lines of Lawson's* Independence. *It is scow-shaped at both bow and stern, but does not pound the water in rough weather as did the Boston boat. Her hull is broad and shallow, while that of* Shamrock III *is comparatively speaking, narrow and deep. The British yacht, like the* Reliance, *has a scow stern, but the bow is like the half of a cone that has been cut lengthwise.*[9]

The fact that the racing yachts carry so much canvas is not the result of chance or mere whim on the part of the constructors. In the building of these yachts, the effect of every extra inch of sail has been calculated with mathematical exactness. Years of experience and a vast amount of experiment have proved that the light, more or less scow-shaped and comparatively broad and shallow hull offers the least resistance to the water. The Herreshoffs have adopted the English idea of very deep keels loaded with lead, which balance the weight of the gigantic masts and sails and the wind pressure against them. Strength, however, has been sacrificed to speed, and the towering steel masts of both *Reliance* and *Shamrock III* were broken early in the season.

L. Francis Herreshoff wrote the following about his father, Captain Nat:

> *At the time* Reliance *was designed her designer was fifty-four years old and perhaps at the peak of his genius. Even then she would not have been possible if Mr. Herreshoff had not had his own very complete yacht building establishment and sail loft manned by a picked crew whom he had trained to be particularly skillful workmen.* Reliance *cost $175,000.00, but it is very doubtful if she could be duplicated for one million today [1963] for there was a lot of manual work on her—such as beautiful forgings and hand finished castings that it would be nearly impossible to find people to make now.*

THE *RESOLUTE*, 1920

The launch of the *Resolute* was noted in the April 25, 1914 issue of the *New York Times*:

> *BRISTOL, R.I., April 24. The bronze sloop yacht* Resolute, *which six present and past flag officers of the New York Yacht Club will offer as a defender of the America's Cup, is near enough to completion to warrant her being launched at sunset tomorrow. She will be rigged speedily and go into commission for her first trial sail probably in ten days, or about the time that the other two defenders are ready for launching.*
>
> *In recognition of their four months' work on the yacht, the draughtsman, metal workers, riveters and riggers were guests at a dinner tonight by Robert W. Emmons, 2d., of Boston, the manager of the* Resolute, *representing the owners. Mr. Emmons formally thanked the workmen.*
>
> *The* Resolute *has been built for Vice Commodore George F. Baker, Jr., Rear Commodore J.P. Morgan, former Commodores F.G. Bourne, Cornelius*

Vanderbilt, and A.C. James, and former Vice Commodore Henry Walters. Secretary George A. Cormack of the New York Yacht Club is secretary of the syndicate and will sail on the yacht with Mr. Emmons. Another amateur, Charles Francis Adams, 2d., Treasurer of Harvard College and one of the most experienced helmsmen on the coast, will handle the boat.

The Resolute *was laid down on Dec. 12, but work was suddenly stopped on the 20th on account, it was said, of a change in the plans. It was resumed six days later and has progressed steadily since then.*

As in the case of the other cup defense yachts constructed at the Herreshoff works, a great deal of secrecy regarding the plans has prevailed. In line with this policy, the Resolute *will be launched as were the* Columbia, Constitution, *and* Reliance, *in the fading twilight. As an additional precaution against revealing her lines, the* Resolute *will slide down greased ways like a battleship, instead of being lowered into the water in a cradle.*

Her rating will be announced before the first races with the other defenders, in order that the time allowance may be reckoned, but her dimensions will be withheld. It is understood that the Resolute *is an enlargement of the fifty-foot sloops, nine of which were built last year by the Herreshoffs for members of the New York Yacht Club.*

The *Resolute* lost the first two matches in the series of five races to the *Shamrock IV*. This was the first time in the history of the races that a challenger had won a race without the defending yacht breaking down. *Period postcard.*

It is reported that the Resolute *is smaller than the other two cup candidates, and may obtain an allowance from the* Defiance *of five minutes in a thirty-mile race.*

The planned 1914 Cup races were interrupted for twelve years because of the European war. This time span would seem to have advantaged the potential American defenders—allowing ample time to design, build and tune their vessels. Three yachts were built to compete for the honor of defending the Cup: the *Defiance*, *Vanitie* and *Resolute*; all were slightly under seventy-five feet waterline length.

The *Defiance* was the concept of George Owen, a professor of naval architecture at MIT. She was built piece by piece by several subcontractors; William Gardner designed the *Vanitie*, and she was built by the George Lawley boat yard in Boston. The third contender, the *Resolute*, was the sixth Cup defender designed and built by Captain Nat Herreshoff, who enjoyed the great advantage of having his design built almost entirely in his own yard. L. Francis Herreshoff remarked, "Mr. Herreshoff was sixty years old when *Resolute* was built, and seventy-two years old the year she defended the Cup."

Consensus between competing yacht clubs on both sides of the Atlantic was about the need to make the competing boats less expensive and less complicated and the racing more competitive, thereby opening the competition to yacht clubs with fewer wealthy members able to finance the design and construction of very expensive racers. It was at the urging of the New York Yacht Club that Captain Nat devised the Universal Rule, the plan that took into consideration Sir Thomas's proposal to limit waterline length to seventy-five feet.

Until the 1920 series, competitors were not required to conform to an identical design formula, and the contenders varied greatly in their measurements; therefore, handicaps were employed in an attempt to make the contestants equal. The 1920 contenders were built to Herreshoff's Universal Rule, attempting to make both challenger and defender uniform, seaworthy and practical. However, there were still differences, and time allowances were applied for the last time in the history of the matches.

Spectators at the fourteenth challenge for the America's Cup watched Lipton's *Shamrock IV* come to within a whisper of taking the Cup back to Britain. After losing the first two races to Lipton's racer, Captain Nat, now seventy-two years old, was rushed to New York; he and skipper Charles Francis Adams worked feverishly making adjustments to *Resolute*'s rig, which evidently unleashed the full potential of Captain Nat's brilliant Cup defender. The *Resolute* lived up to her name and won the final three matches in the series of five races.

For Captain Nat, 1920 marked the end of a thirty-seven-year winning streak during which his innovative and graceful designs had kept the America's Cup safe in its New York Yacht Club home. As one of the yachting fraternity's most revered and inventive designers, Nathanael Greene Herreshoff left his unmistakable fingerprints on the sport of sailing. He designed more than two thousand vessels propelled by steam power and wind power. Adding to Captain Nat's six Cup-winning designs, the Herreshoff Manufacturing Company built two additional defenders, one in 1930 and another in 1934.

THE *ENTERPRISE*, 1930

The *Enterprise*, a 121-foot J-class sloop designed by W. Starling Burgess, was built by the Herreshoff Manufacturing Company when the boat yard was under the management of Bristol's Haffenreffer family. The 1930 Cup defender was big! Owned by the Aldrich Syndicate, the *Enterprise* was 80 feet on the waterline with an overall length of 120 feet; she displaced 128 tons and carried 7,583 square feet of sail. The so-called Park Avenue boom

The J-class yacht *Enterprise* is shown in 1930 in Herreshoff's south shop just prior to her launching.

The *Enterprise*'s hollow mast is being worked on by yard hands and crew members. The *Enterprise*'s mast was 152 feet tall; she had spreaders for support and carried much steel cable rigging.

was first used on the *Enterprise*. Her original spruce mast was replaced with a circular section double-skin duralumin mast; her hull was plated with Tobin bronze, and she pioneered the use of retractable spreaders. *Enterprise* easily won four straight races with Lipton's *Shamrock V*, thereby adding more laurels to the Herreshoff name.

THE *RAINBOW*, 1934

In 1934, sooner than expected, Thomas O.M. Sopwith,[10] an experienced British yachtsman, made a new challenge. He commissioned Charles E. Nicholson to design and build the first *Endeavour.*

As with the Watson-designed *Shamrock II* in 1901, which was the first boat to be designed following numerous towing-tank tests, the William Starling

Burgess–designed *Rainbow* was the first J to be conceived according to the same principles: during two months in 1931, at the tank-test facilities at the University of Michigan, dozens of models were tested by Burgess.

The *Rainbow*, a formable speedster, was launched from the Herreshoff yards on May 15, 1934. Her hull was Tobin bronze below the waterline over steel frames and steel above the waterline; her mast was duralumin, boom and spinnaker wood; her waterline length was 82 feet, overall length 127 feet, 7 inches, displacement 141 tons and sail spread was 7,535 square feet.

The challenger *Endeavour* was a faster boat than the defender. The *Endeavour* won the first two races in the best four of seven series, and she was ahead in the third race when she ran into calm air. Tactical errors kept her from winning that race and the three that followed.

Superb sail handling by *Rainbow*'s crew of thirty-one, and expert strategy on the part of Skipper Harold Vanderbilt, brought the *Rainbow* through to victory. The New York Yacht Club's 1934 Cup defender, winner of the fifteenth America's Cup challenge, defeated *Endeavour* by four wins to two.

The owner syndicate, organized by Harold S. Vanderbilt, was joined by these gentlemen of capital: Frederick W. Vanderbilt, William K. Vanderbilt, Alfred G. Vanderbilt, J.P. Morgan, Gerard B. Lambert, Marshall Field, Edward S. Harkness, George F. Baker Jr., Charles Hayden, George E. Roosevelt, W.G. McCullough, Joseph P. Day, Henry H. Rogers, Walter P. Chrysler, Ogden L. Mills, Alfred P. Sloane Jr. and Winthrop W. Aldrich.

After the 1934 America's Cup win, the *Rainbow* was laid up in dry dock for two years in Bristol, where she was later refitted by Vanderbilt for use as a trial horse. She was sold to Chandler Hovey in 1937 to race the defender selection trials, but the *Ranger* eliminated her. *Rainbow* was again laid up at the end of 1937 at Herreshoff's Bristol yard and came to an ignominious end in 1940 when she was sold for scrap.

Chapter 9
The *Shamrock* Challengers
(1899–1930)

The challenge of Sir Thomas Lipton for the 1899 match revived good international feelings. Lipton's boat, the *Shamrock*, was built by William Fife, Watson's principal competitor, who turned out some of the fastest yachts in English waters. On our side, the Herreshoffs built a fast new boat for C. Oliver Iselin and Commodore J. Pierpont Morgan, the *Columbia*.

According to the *Scientific American* dated July 8, 1899, there were many rumors regarding the *Shamrock*. There was none more improbable than the statement that the English boat was to carry a centerboard. The fate of the centerboard, as far as big yachts were concerned, was determined in 1893, when the keel boat *Valkyrie II* easily vanquished the centerboard *Vigilant* in a fifteen-mile rush to windward against a stiff breeze. The *Valkyrie II* was the first of the ninety-footers to be built upon the fin-keel principle, just as the *Vigilant* was the last of the ninety-footers to carry a centerboard.

In 1895, the Herreshoffs abandoned the centerboard in favor of the fixed keel. The *Defender* was the first keel single-stick yacht built for the defense of the Cup. Therefore, it was not likely that Fife would return to a form of construction that had been abandoned by the people who so long used it and so thoroughly understood its possibilities.

On the subject of keels and centerboards, it is satisfactory to know that the *Columbia*, in the few trials that she had with the *Defender*, had shown, even before she had time to be "tuned up," that she was a somewhat faster boat. The difference was not remarkable, but it was obvious, and those who may

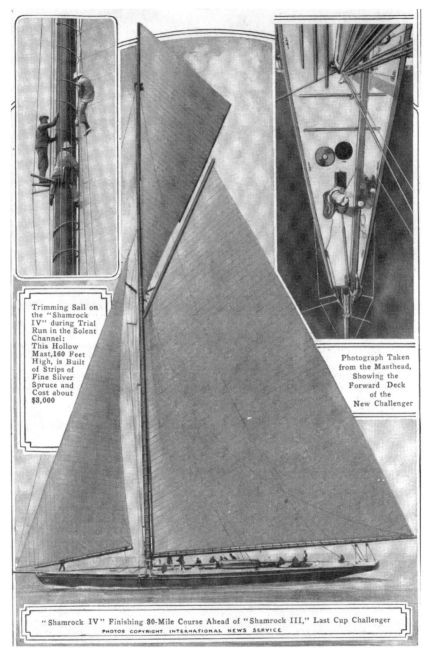

Trimming Sail on the "Shamrock IV" during Trial Run in the Solent Channel; This Hollow Mast, 160 Feet High, is Built of Strips of Fine Silver Spruce and Cost about $3,000

Photograph Taken from the Masthead, Showing the Forward Deck of the New Challenger

"Shamrock IV" Finishing 30-Mile Course Ahead of "Shamrock III," Last Cup Challenger

PHOTOS COPYRIGHT INTERNATIONAL NEWS SERVICE

In this 1920 photo montage by the International News Service, Sir Thomas Lipton's *Shamrock IV* is seen in three aspects: (left) crew members are trimming the sail during her trial run in the Solent; (right) this photo, taken from the masthead, shows the forward deck of the new Cup challenger; (center) the *Shamrock IV* is finishing a thirty-mile race ahead of Lipton's previous challenger, *Shamrock III*.

have felt disappointed that she had not shown a more marked superiority must surely have remembered that it was more difficult to make a gain of five minutes over a thirty-mile course in the present era (1899) of yacht designing than it had been to make one of fifteen or twenty minutes a dozen years earlier. In competitive trials between the new and old Cup defenders, we must remember that *Defender* was a phenomenally fast boat. Now, *Columbia* would probably have about five minutes' advantage of *Defender* on a thirty-mile course and therefore be taken to be from twenty to twenty-five minutes better than the last Fife ninety-foot yacht.

The *Shamrock*, the sixth British cutter seeking to capture the America's Cup, was making her way across the Atlantic when the weekly *Scientific American* newspaper dated August 12, 1899, wrote of the interest to compare this new challenger's sailing qualities against previous British yachts that had made the same quest. "It is a right royal line with which this Anglo-Scotch-Irish craft is associated in holding her title of challenger; and with her Irish name, Scotch design, and English construction, she is truly representative of the people to whose fostering care the early growth of the sport of yacht sailing and its present popularity are largely due."

Sir Tom's first challenge for the Cup came with the *Shamrock* seen here tuning up in the Solent. *Period postcard.*

The *Shamrock II* is viewed going through her paces. *Period postcard.*

In the dimensions and construction of both defender and challenger there was great similarity. The *Columbia*, though stronger than the *Defender*, was a remarkably light craft, and in the *Shamrock*, Thorneycroft, with his quarter of a century experience building torpedo boats, produced a hull and spars that were probably an advance over Herreshoff's boat in the matter of light scantling up-to-the-limit construction. *Shamrock's* builders kept the boat's underwater shape shrouded in secrecy, no doubt endeavoring to conceal her excessive draft; wise observers suggested it not unlikely that she would be found to draw as much as twenty-two feet. This would mean lower lead, less of it and a nearer approach to the true fin keel than had been shown in any ninety-foot yacht since the construction of the *Pilgrim* in 1893.

Scientific American continues:

> A study of the two vessels [reveal] notable differences in their sail plans. Shamrock's mast appears to be stepped about 2 feet further aft than Columbia's, and her bowsprit is considerably longer, the distance from mast to outer end of bowsprit being from 5 to 7 feet grater in Shamrock. Her present boom is about the same length as Columbia's. The gaff,

topmast, and hoist of mainsail, on the other hand, are a few feet less than Columbia*'s, so that the sail plan is longer on the base line but not as lofty as that of the American boat. She probably carries a larger spinnaker, larger head sails, and a similar mainsail, the effect of which, other things being equal, should be to give* Columbia *the advantage in windward work and* Shamrock *in reaching and running. Her owner, Sir Thomas Lipton, and her designer, "Willie" Fife, have both stated that she is to carry a larger mainsail in the races on this side.*

The first race took place on October 3 in the presence of the largest spectator fleet yet assembled. Neither Lipton nor Morgan sailed aboard their racing yachts; rather, they enjoyed the spectacle from their palatial steam yachts.

THE *SHAMROCK II*, 1901

The weekly journal *Scientific American*, dated May 25, 1901, relates some of the characteristics of the *Shamrock II*. The paper's reporter wrote that particular interest was attached to the trial outings of the new Cup racer, insofar as her designer, George Lennox Watson, applied modern scientific

Shamrock II is tuning in a trial race against *Shamrock* in the Solent. *Period postcard.*

principles to her creation. The new boat's dimensions were very compatible with those of the *Columbia*.

> *By all the calculations it appeared likely that the new craft would be excessively tender, and the fact that the scanty rail with which she is provided is put eighteen inches inside the point at which the deck and topsides meet, suggests that the designer himself expected that she would heel far and easily in anything of a breeze. The fine-drawn quarters were opposed only on the ground that the want of beam there robbed the yacht of much of her power to carry sail, and this danger of having a boat which might prove unable to stand up to her work in moderate breeze was intensified by the shallower draught, less beam, steeper floor and greater height of sail plan given to* Shamrock II, *as compare with previous challengers.*
>
> *In subsequent trials between the 1899* Shamrock *and the 1901* Shamrock II, *it was reported the current challenger was beaten by her predecessor in a strong breeze and rough sea by more than five minutes, the older boat showing superiority on every point of sailing.*
>
> *These calculations looked sound, but they are contradicted in practice, for a careful observation extending through the whole of the first two days' trials shows the new challenger to be able to stand up to a breeze better than* Shamrock *and that she inclines to stiffness rather than to tenderness.*
>
> *It is offered in explanation that the sails of* Shamrock II *were ill-fitting particularly the mainsail, and that she was not in proper trim. Although this is probably true, it cannot be denied that the race has been somewhat of a disappointment in England, and also in America, where the interest is always greatly heightened if the challenger is believed to be a dangerous boat. The last race was over a 30-mile course the difference would have been about 8 minutes.* Columbia *beat* [the first] Shamrock *in a very similar wind and sea by 6 minutes and 31 seconds, and* Constitution *will probably be 4 or 5 minutes better than* Columbia.[11] *This shows the challenger to be many minutes slower than she should be, if the cup is to be carried back to the Solent.*

Returning to L. Francis Herreshoff's take on the 1901 Cup race, we learn that Herreshoff commended Watson's design of the *Shamrock II*; he said that because the Irish boat was slightly larger than the *Columbia* and carried about eight hundred square feet more canvas she had to allow a forty-three-second handicap to the defender.

The first race on September 28 was a thirty-mile windward-leeward course in which the challenger held a very slight lead most of the time to

In this illustration, the *Shamrock II* and the *Columbia* are seen running neck to neck. Herreshoff's *Columbia* won 3–0 over *Shamrock II*. *Period postcard.*

windward and rounded the weather mark with a forty-one-second lead. Spectators familiar with smaller skimming dish yachts expected the *Shamrock II* to run away from the *Columbia* in the run to leeward, but the narrower *Columbia*, with comparatively sharp bow, surprised many when she overtook and passed the *Shamrock II* just before crossing the finish line thirty-five seconds ahead.

The second race, which was started on October 1, was called off for lack of wind, and it appeared the race could not be completed within the allotted time. However, *Shamrock II* did show her power by rounding the first weather mark first.

The second try to run the second race got off on October 3. A much stronger wind from the northwest of ten to twelve knots with stronger puffs later proved to be perfect for the bout. L. Francis Herreshoff praises Barr's tactical skill:

> *It was a triangular course and I guess Charlie Barr thought he had rather poor chances under these conditions if he were interfered with by what was supposed to be the fastest yacht on a reach, so, after luffing* Shamrock II *over the line before time, so that she would have to recross the mark and lose time, he waited until nearly the time of the second gun and started with*

Shamrock II lost to Herreshoff's *Columbia*. *Period postcard.*

good way on so that under these conditions he had a chance to win with
Columbia*'s handicap without actually catching up with* Shamrock II.

The third and final race of the match got off at 11:00 a.m. on October 4
for a leeward and windward course. Both yachts, not wanting to be blanked

by the other in the downwind start, hung back. At the two-minute warning, both went over the line at practically the same time.

L. Francis Herreshoff wrote that the wind at the start was from the northwest at about ten knots. He said that when the yachts tacked to the west, the wind coming off the Jersey shore was more westerly and with a little more velocity. In that situation, both yachts, one after the other, took the lead and then lost the lead. "Captain Barr, with his iron nerves, sailed *Columbia* best in the last few miles of the race."

The "old" *Columbia* beat the brand-new *Shamrock II* in spite of the latter's more modern and scientific design by George Lennox Watson. The talent of Skipper Charlie Barr made the difference, because the performance of Sir Thomas's green-colored boat was nevertheless excellent.

For spectators, this was the most exciting race of the series. The yachts swapped the lead and lost it several times, but in the run to leeward the *Shamrock II* proved to be the fastest boat and in the last part of the run established a major lead.

THE *SHAMROCK III*, 1903

In 1903, Irish tea merchant Sir Thomas Lipton made his third attempt, in five years, to take the Cup back to Britain. He hired William Fife to design a yacht, the result of which was the *Shamrock III*. The *Scientific American* dated June 27, 1903, published the following account about Lipton's new challenger:

> Shamrock III *is a marked departure, in some respects from any challenger that has been sent over from the other side for many years past. We have to go back to* Valkyrie II *to find a midship section that bears any similarity to the easy bilges and full garboards that distinguish* Shamrock III *so sharply from any of her immediate predecessors, and in this respect she is the more wholesome yacht of any of the existing challengers and defenders of the 90 foot class.*
>
> *The overall length of* Shamrock III *is close to 140 feet, the waterline length slightly under 90 feet; beam about 25 feet 6 inches—not 22 feet 6 inches, as reported by a cablegram sent out by the builders of the boat; draft in racing trim 21 feet, and her displacement in the neighborhood of 150 tons. Although her midship section is large, the lines, which have been carried out with the skill that characterizes all the Fife boats, are so sweet*

Shamrock III was humbled by the Herreshoff-designed *Reliance*. *Period postcard.*

and fair that she looks at first glance more like a 70-footer than a boat built up to the full 90 foot limit. The sections throughout are round and fair, free from sudden changes of curve or "humps." "Round as a barrel" is the term that may justly be applied to Shamrock III. *She should show small initial stability—a valuable feature when the wind is light and the sea troubled—while her deep and easy bilges will give her great sail carrying power when she is heeled to her best sailing lines.*

Sir Thomas, when referring to his third attempt to win the Cup, said, "You could not say I went into this hazard of challenging for the America's Cup on a hasty impulse." When in dry dock in a Brooklyn, New York boatyard, the *Shamrock III*, with all her shrouds removed, revealed her fine lines. She measured 134 feet overall, 9 feet shorter than the *Reliance*, and she had a fuller, deeper body. By popular consensus, she was the finest cutter ever built in Britain. (It was reported that the *Shamrock III* was much faster than the *Shamrock*, but it must be remembered that the same thing was said of *Shamrock II* in 1901—a statement that did not hold water.) After people got a good look at *Shamrock III*, they began to believe she had a chance at victory.

The races by these giant sloops, with long overhang at bow and stern and their tremendous expanse of sail, must have been a thrill to witness. *Reliance* captured all three races. *Shamrock III*, getting lost in fog, withdrew during the third race; rather than finishing the race, she set her course for shore.

THE *SHAMROCK IV*, 1920

Lipton challenged again in 1914 under the new rating rule. However, World War I interrupted plans to build yachts for the challenge and defense, so the Cup was safe in the halls of the New York Yacht Club for the duration.

Plans came together in 1920 for the long-anticipated match, and the Cup was up for grabs once again. Lipton brought out *Shamrock IV* to meet another Herreshoff creation, the *Resolute*.

Charles Nicholson, *Shamrock*'s designer, included a fatal error in his design when it called for a waterline of 4 feet (110 feet, 4 inches) greater than *Resolute* (106 feet, 4 inches), which meant she had to carry more sail than the *Resolute*, therefore allowing her adversary as much as seven minutes, fifteen seconds handicap.

In the opening match on July 15, the *Resolute* was forced to resign the race after an error in sail handling; her mainsail halyard broke, thereby allowing *Shamrock IV* the win. The second race took place on July 20, and Lipton's yacht won it by two minutes, twenty-six seconds, corrected time.

Faced with the third and possibly final race, and loss of the Cup, Captain Nat was whisked overnight aboard a U.S. Navy destroyer to make adjustments

The First World War and other events left a gap in challenges until Lipton, on his *Shamrock IV*, raced against Herreshoff's last Cup boat, the *Resolute*, losing 3–2. This image is from a period magic lantern slide.

to the *Resolute*'s rig. Captain Nat intimately knew his design and tweaked her to be the unbridled champion he had created.

In race three, on the windward-leeward course, following a demanding nineteen tacks, the *Resolute* held the lead. However, the *Shamrock IV*, a powerful racer skippered by professional Captain William Burton, fought back, and the racers crossed the finish line in a dead heat. The committee gave the win to the *Resolute* on a corrected time of seven minutes, one second. The margins of *Resolute*'s victories increased in the next two races, in which she proved herself the faster boat with a crew who worked with military-like correctness. The *Resolute* successfully defended the Cup with a 3–2 victory on July 27 with a corrected time win of nineteen minutes, forty-five seconds.

THE *SHAMROCK V*, 1930

The *Shamrock V* was Sir Tom's fifth and final attempt to capture the America's Cup. She was designed by Charles Nicholson and built in the Camper & Nicholson yard in Gasport, Hampshire, England; she was the first British yacht built to the J-Class Rule. *Shamrock V* was sturdily built: mahogany planking over steel frames, yellow pine deck, teak used for stem and stern posts and counter-timbers and hollow spruce mast. She had lower sail area but greater rig height relative to other 1930 Js. She was extensively tuned in England before the races. Her vital statistics are no less impressive: her waterline length was 81 feet, 1 inch; overall length 119 feet, 8 inches; she displaced 134 tons; and her sail area was slightly less than *Enterprise* at 7,540 square feet.

The yacht continued being modified after launch—her hull shape and rudder were changed, as was her rig, to create the most effective racing sail plan.

Geoffrey F. Hammond, in his *Showdown at Newport*, writes, "The Cup match itself was a rout, the worst defeat suffered by any of Sir Thomas Lipton's five challengers. Aboard his power yacht *Erin*, the 82-year old Lipton watched what he knew was his last chance dissolving before his tired eyes."

Chapter 10
The Js, 12-Metres and the IACC Yachts

We must look upon the modern racing yacht as an important, as well as a curious, production. She is as much a result of high breeding as a race horse. Indeed, it is difficult to feel that this splendid creature, with her all but human beauty, her fragilities, and her foibles, is really inanimate. A yachtsman will trace the pedigree of his favorite racer back through Gloriana, Puritan, *and* Magic, *and name the exact points of excellence which she has obtained from each.*
—Ray Stannard Baker, October 1899

UNIVERSAL RULE AND J-BOATS: 1920–1937

The J-class was the culmination of the big boats—they were the maxi-yachts of their day. There was always a loose grouping of big racing yachts that formed the pinnacle of the sport of yacht racing from the mid-1800s to the beginning of World War II. Between 1930 and 1937, ten J-class yachts were built, four in Britain and six in the United States, principally as competitors for the America's Cup in 1930, 1934 and 1937.

The J's designers—people like Sir Charles Nicholson, the young Olin Stephens, aircraft manufacturer Thomas O.M. Sopwith and his chief engineer, Frank Murdock—drew heavily from the latest steel technology. They also borrowed ideas from the burgeoning aerospace industry.

When the greatest J-class yacht, the *Ranger*, tacked, she made a sound "like distant thunder," wrote an admirer. Their mainsails of Egyptian cotton weighed a ton, and that was before the wind loaded them up further. The

The J-class defender yacht *Enterprise* is seen in trials prior the 1930 races. The boats of the J-class series came out in 1930 with masts as tall as 165 feet and over 80 feet in length. Vanderbilt's *Enterprise* met Lipton's *Shamrock V* in Rhode Island Sound winning 4–0. *Associated Press*.

The 1934 J-class challenger *Endeavour. Period postcard.*

The 1930 Cup defender, the J-class yacht *Ranger*. What distinguished the J-boats were their size and the technology. They weren't just big; they were clever. The *Ranger* is seen here on a period postcard; she beat *Endeavour II* in their 1937 match.

main sheet alone of Lipton's *Shamrock V* stretched ninety fathoms and required a score of deckhands to close-haul the boom. The winches on the *Ranger* were as big around as five-gallon drums, and the 60-foot-long spinnaker poles were as thick as a man's chest. The job of hoisting the 10,000-square-foot parachute spinnakers required the sweating services of fifteen bull-strength men. The J's masts were 160 feet high, and only daily maintenance kept them upright.

And so they thundered along. Though she wasn't good enough to defend the Cup, the U.S. J-boat *Yankee* once charged up a ten-mile windward leg at an average speed of 13.25 knots, carving out a bow wave of boiling water that sluiced down her flush decks like a torrent. Woe to any crewman who got caught in it; he would be swept straight off the boat.

The fourteen-story high masts almost defied gravity and the spar maker's art. The twelve-sided mast on Vanderbilt's 1930 defender, the *Enterprise*, was fashioned in rolled plate, joined with eighty thousand rivets and welded. It was an engineering tour de force that weighed only two tons, compared with *Shamrock V*'s 6,250-pound wooden stick.

Technically, the J-boats were right on the leading edge. Aircraft pioneer T.O.M. Sopwith's *Endeavour*, which was years ahead of her time, boasted four-speed winches and a forerunner of today's wind gauges. Other J-class innovations foreshadowed, by decades, modern sailing trends. They number the famed "Park Avenue" boom,[12] composite hull construction, stripped-out interiors, rod rigging, coffee-grinder winches, formal tank testing and parachute spinnakers.

Oddly, the Js were never conceived as yachts to last through the ages; they represented the state-of-the-art in racing craft, designed to be replaced after a season or two. The staggering beauty and elegant low hulls, 160-foot-high masts and remarkable power under sail have lead to the most improbable end of all—their rescue and admiration some sixty years later.[13]

Until the 1920 series, contenders were not required to conform to an identical design formula, and the competing yachts varied greatly in dimensions. Therefore, handicaps had to be given in an attempt to equalize competitors. In the 1920s, racers for the America's Cup were built according to the Universal Rating Rule in an attempt to make all contestants the same. However, as you read in Chapter 8, the nonconforming *Shamrock IV* had to give a time allowance to the *Reliance*. The 1920 match was the last one in which handicaps were given.

The world's yachting alliance, which kept a hungry eye upon the premier international yacht-racing trophy, sighed heavily at the tremendous expense that the design and building of a Cup challenger had become. The New

Enthusiastic yachtsmen had judged the dark blue-hulled *Endeavour II*, only slightly smaller than the *Ranger*, a more attractive vessel. In this June 1937 photo, T.O.M. Sopwith is trying out his two sloops; he is aboard his *Endeavour* with his *Endeavour II* in the background. *Associated Press.*

York Yacht Club and potential builders of Cup defenders felt that huge yachts such as the *Independence* and *Reliance* were too expensive, complicated and potentially dangerous. Halsey C. Herreshoff, a marine architect and grandson of Captain Nat, authored the following as an Internet file titled "A History of America's Cup Racing":

> *They* [members of the New York Yacht Club] *turned to Captain Nat Herreshoff to devise a new rule to provide good competitive racing with reasonable freedom of design but with more "normal" boats. Actually, Mr. Herreshoff had been analyzing the problem for nearly a decade previously.*
>
> *His solution was the "Universal Rule." One appeal of this rule was its simple physical validity: length and sail area in the numerator are speed-giving elements while displacement in the denominator is a retarding quantity. Also the rule is dimensionally correct in that length times the square root of sail area divided by the cube root of displacement is a linear measurement as "rating" should be.*
>
> *Mr. Herreshoff's invention of "quarter beam length" as an element of the measured length taken at two heights assessed more properly the sailing length of the yacht than did just a set of lengths taken on center. The Universal Rule was indeed about universally accepted. But for the change of the overall coefficient and addition of detailed controls, this rule was used for the rest of the big boat America's Cup racing.*
>
> *Sir Thomas Lipton, who had cheerfully financed challenge after challenge, felt that the boats should be smaller. It was he who first proposed a challenge in smaller yachts built to the Universal Rule; in 1912 he formalized the proposal for 75 ft waterline boats rather than the 90-Footers of the previous era. The New York Yacht Club at first refused, and then accepted this practical challenge by Lipton.*
>
> *After that, further refinements of the yachts, and the J-Class sloop of 76 foot rating was agreed upon. This event was the beginning of the Marconi mainsail, the rig which omitted gaffs, topsails and overhanging booms; thus both challenger and defender were designed to the same rating formula.*
>
> *The J boat era of 1930 could be called the Vanderbilt era. Harold S. Vanderbilt was skipper in 1930, 1934 and 1937. He was also the principal backer of the magnificent Js,* Enterprise, Rainbow, *and* Ranger, *financing the latter entirely himself. In 1934, the Cup was again nearly lost. It is generally believed that* Rainbow *was not as fast as the challenger* Endeavor *and that the* Rainbow *won through the acumen of Vanderbilt and C. Sherman Hoyt of his afterguard.*

Ranger *was the first Cup Defender in fifty years not built at the Herreshoff Manufacturing Company in Bristol. She is nearly always described as the "super J" and that accolade seems to have been totally deserved. Here was a clear demonstration of the axiom "build big within the rule." Except for L. Francis Herreshoff's* Whirlwind, *no boat had previously approached the maximum size practical for a rating of 76 under the modified Universal Rule;* Ranger *did.*

Nathanael Greene Herreshoff III, writing in the 2001 *Herreshoff Marine Museum Chronicle*, relates his memories of the majestic Js and the so-called Peacock Alley on Bristol's lower Hope Street:

In the history of the America's Cup, the J-boat era began in 1930, the year before I was born. Two potential cup defenders were built that year by the Herreshoff Manufacturing Company, the Enterprise *designed by*

High and dry at the Herreshoff yard in Bristol, Rhode Island, the triumphant Cup defender the *Ranger* rests on her laurels. *Associated Press.*

Starling Burgess, son of Edward Burgess, and the Weetamoe *designed by Clinton Crane. Two additional cup contenders were built at Lawley's yard in Boston, the* Yankee *designed by Frank Paine and the* Whirlwind *designed by my uncle L. Francis Herreshoff, son of Captain Nat. Two earlier cup boats, the* Resolute *and the* Vanitie, *were used that year as trial horses to determine which contender would defend the Cup. The*

In this photo taken in his Bristol boat yard about 1905, Captain Nat addresses his son A. Sidney DeWolf Herreshoff.

Enterprise *was the winner. It is interesting to note that the 1930 Cup races were held for the first time off Newport, and Sir Thomas Lipton challenged for the fifth and final time in* Shamrock V *and then proceeded to lose to* Enterprise.

My grandfather, Captain Halsey Chase, took me to the launching of the Rainbow *on May 15, 1934, a foggy, rainy day. In the very crowded south shop Mrs. Gertrude Vanderbilt christened this famous yacht. On the same morning, the Nantucket Light Ship, in a similar fog, was rammed and sunk by the ocean liner* Olympic.

Several months later, on the morning of August 8th, I went with my parents, Sid and Becky Herreshoff, and some guests on my father's launch, the Bubble, *to meet the blue hulled British challenger, the* Endeavour, *coming up Narragansett Bay. She was under tow by T.O.M. Sopwith's motor yacht, the* Vita. *The* Endeavour, *rigged as a yawl, had made the crossing from Gosport, England under tow in sixteen days. I did not attend any of the cup races that year but remember hearing about them from my parents who were spectators.*

In 1935, I recall seeing the 1930 winner, the Enterprise, *being scrapped at the yard. Much of her gear was then used on both* Rainbow *and* Ranger. *Both* Rainbow *and* Weetamoe *were raced in the 1936 season. I can remember climbing up a long ladder to board* Rainbow *while she was hauled for maintenance. I also remember an evening after the season was over seeing* Rainbow *going down the bay on her way to Bath, Maine to have her gear transferred to the new cup defender,* Ranger.

In the spring of 1937, Ranger *arrived at the Herreshoff yard after much of her mast had broken off on the way to Bristol. The* Rainbow *returned, painted gray under new ownership, to be refurbished using some of* Weetamoe's *gear.* Endeavour I *and* Endeavour II *were also at the yard being tuned up after their ocean crossings.*

On separate occasions during the 1937 season we had two famous luncheon guests at our home. One was Harold Vanderbilt, skipper of three America's Cup defenders during the J-boat era. The other was designer Olin Stephens' brother, Rod, serving as one of the Ranger's *crew.*

That season we went out of Newport in the Bubble *several times to watch a few of the Cup races. After the season, a number of these cup boats were lined along Hope Street one after another. This section of Hope Street came to be known as "Peacock Alley" in honor of these beautiful, famous racers. Going from north to south, these magnificent yachts were in the following order (listed with the dates they were scrapped):* Resolute *(1938),* Vanitie *(1939),* Ranger *(1941), and the* Weetamoe *(1938).*

The dismantling of these beautiful racing machines began in 1938, and the days of the racing Js passed into history.

THE 12-METRE ERA: 1958–1987

Indeed, the 12-metre yachts represent the longest period in which any single design has ruled Cup racing. The 12-metre era, which grew out of the European-based International Rule, ran for nearly thirty years. At their introduction, 12-metres had the merit of keeping down costs because they were half the size of the J-class. Economy was, in fact, the main reason for their introduction.

Thus, the 12-metre era was born from two factors: a shortage of finance and a shortage of challengers. Many people believed that the America's Cup era had died with the unrepeatable J-class and World War I. It was hoped that the less expensive and simpler 12-metres, which were not required as before to sail to the race site on their own bottoms, would stimulate new interest in challenging for the Cup. Clearly, that did happen. But it is now acknowledged that the 12-metre rule finally developed almost to its ultimate. The 12-metres, allowed in the Cup when the Deed of Gift's minimum length rule was lowered from sixty to forty-four feet by the New York Yacht Club, were the answer.

Victory in these same-looking yachts depended on tiny and usually invisible improvements in rig and hull. It has been written by sportswriters that the 12-metre was "recherché class," or over-refined. The class produced three of the most famous America's Cup boats: Intrepid won in both 1967 and 1970; Courageous won in 1974 and 1977 and was sailed in the 1986 Louis Vuitton Cup; and Alan Bond's *Australia II* broke the New York Yacht Club's 132-year hold on the Cup with its innovative winged keel in 1983.

Some have argued that only two new elements have stirred worldwide interest in the Cup again. One was the winged keel on the Australia II and the other was the windy 1987 Fremantle venue. The boat has remained essentially the same. To laypeople, all 12-metres look alike.

In design terms, the 12-metre, though graceful in tradition of European narrow-beamed sloops, is dated. It has a non-planing displacement hull underneath a modern rig, which makes for enormous loads on the rig in windy conditions. Though fast upwind, the 12-metre is much slower downwind in a breeze than the modern breed of planing yachts. They do not represent the advanced design thinking (not until KZ7 was made of fiberglass, the advanced use of materials) that typified the big boat challenges.

Halsey C. Herreshoff, grandson of Captain Nat, has written about his experiences aboard Cup defenders:

> *I can write more knowledgeably about the 12-Metre era than any other, as I was an active participant for 25 years and an observer for the full 29 years. Through acquaintance with Harry Sears, I was excused from other duties as a naval officer to sail aboard* Columbia, *the 1958 Cup Defender, as bowman. Sailing aboard the 12s in most of their seasons, I participated in four America's Cup series, a total of 20 races; it was all about the greatest fun I've ever had.*
>
> *The International Rule is an inelegant arbitrary formula that controls and restricts the design of these boats within narrow limits. There is a minimum length, maximum draft, maximum rig heights, and a set relation between length and displacement. Scantlings first in wood and later in aluminum are tightly controlled by specifics of the rule, Nevertheless, innovation in design particularly by Olin Stephens brought about nearly continual improvement of the boats, and the design edge of the United States long seemed to assure retention of the Cup as it did over many matches through 1980.*

The 1958 match contested the *Columbia*, sailed by Briggs Cunningham and designed by Sparkman & Stephens, against the British yacht *Sceptre*, G. Mann, skipper. Halsey rated the five-race series with this remark: "The Cup race itself that year was a walk; *Sceptre* was a quite inferior design that had never faced competition before the match."

The 1962 challenge was won by the *Weatherly*. Halsey described the *Weatherly* as "a weak American boat," but she successfully defended the Cup by the brilliance of Bus Mobacher, her skipper. This was the first year an Australian challenger, the *Gretel*, won a race, demonstrating the aggressive posture of Australian sailors.

The *Constellation*, another Sparkman & Stephens design, defended and won in 1964. Halsey describes the *Constellation* as "a quite elegant all-round boat, which was selected as Cup Defender over the large and powerful *American Eagle*, which was only superior in heavy weather. This should have been a tip off to the future but the true significance of having to design the smallest possible 12-Metre for Newport conditions was not generally appreciated until *Australia II* lifted the Cup in 1983."

Olin Stephens's *Intrepid* of 1967 was a breakthrough yacht. Wetted surface was drastically reduced with a shorter keel and separate rudder, and the boat had numerous refinements. With outstanding management and the skill of Bus Mosbacher again as skipper, *Intrepid* was unbeatable. The *Intrepid* again successfully saved the Cup in the 1970 match.

For the 1974 match, Olin Stephens designed the *Courageous*; she was built of aluminum under new scantling rules. Halsey had this comment:

> *The* Courageous *was powerful and superior in a breeze but did not easily defeat* Intrepid, *striving for a third defense. The selection trials reduced to a memorable sudden-death race in a 30-knot northeast breeze that* Courageous *won through both superior speed and better sailing. While I personally believe that Stephens's 1977 boat,* Enterprise, *was a further improvement in the same direction, Ted Turner sailing* Courageous *beat her out for the defense. Though not of demonstrably different dimensions,* Freedom *of 1980 seemed very superior. One difference was lower freeboard—providing a lower center of gravity and less hull windage. The new ingredient was a brilliant program of development of sails, gear and crew established by skipper Dennis Conner over a two-year program. The success of the program altered America's Cup procedures from then on. Even with that,* Freedom *did lose one of the races of the match principally owing to a light-air advantage of Australia employing a rule-beating mainsail that gave her superior windward speed in light air.*

Then, in 1983, the unthinkable happened in Newport when *Australia II* beat *Liberty* in "the Race of the Century," the sudden-death seventh race of that match. *Australia II* was the best 12-metre yacht to sail in the twenty-five-year history of competition at Newport. Her extraordinary and controversial winged keel was, of course, the conspicuous feature. The ballyhoo about that masked the significant facts that *Australia II* was the first boat to go to minimum 12-metre length and displacement and that she had significantly less wetted surface than any other 12; this latter fact won the Cup!

Halsey continues:

> *While the racing ended at Newport in 1983 with the victory by the wonderful* Australia II, *the subsequent events are equally interesting. Dennis Conner took charge again and with a brilliantly conceived and executed plan won back the Cup the first time sailing Twelves in the challenging waters of Western Australia. The final* Stars & Stripes [winning the 1987

match against the *Kookaburra III*] *was a one-weather boat, big and powerful for the consistent "Doctor"* [strong winds] *of Fremantle.*

THE MISMATCH, 1988

In 1988, for the first time in history, the challenger and defender clubs could not agree on a mutually satisfactory boat size, type and rating rule. Thus, it was necessary to sail under an as-yet-untried provision of the Deed of Gift framed for just such a contingency. The result was a fiasco that was not without skill in design and excitement in sailing. On the whole, this year was a disgrace to the noble tradition of the Cup. The match was between a large challenger sloop and a sophisticated large catamaran. The Americans developed the latter over an amazingly short time period. Obviously, such a mismatch would be won by a large margin by one boat or the other. Quite naturally, the catamaran was the winner, even when sailed very conservatively. The perpetrator of the mismatch was Michael Fay of New Zealand. While openly discussing a conventional 12-metre challenge, Fay had secretly commissioned the design and had commenced construction of a large sloop. Then, when he felt he had an insurmountable time lead on the defender, Fay issued a challenge specifying his type of boat and a time period too short for the defender to reasonably develop a boat of the same type.

The San Diego Yacht Club refused and then tried to reason with Fay. This was to no avail. Then, the lawyers got into the act. As is increasingly frequent in our litigious society, the role of competing lawyers and judges was to ensnare the Cup in a miserable, expensive dispute.

In fairness, the American response to being boxed into a corner was not always admirable either. America won, and did so through great technology and clever development of a quite wonderful catamaran, *Stars & Stripes*. But even now one wonders if the whole fiasco might not have been avoided by more negotiation appealing to the common sense of all.

The challenger, *New Zealand*, was a yacht of approximately ninety feet waterline length, making her the largest racing sloop constructed since the J-boats. While developed using modern composite construction, *New Zealand* was a peculiar boat. We have no sure way to judge her prowess, as she was the only such boat on the water. Light of weight with an extreme (model boat type) keel and wide "wings" for crew hiking, she was interesting. The sail plan and sails were equally interesting. Of course, it really made no difference whether *New Zealand* was good or bad, because a good catamaran was sure to beat her every time except in such light air conditions that neither boat would make the time limit.

NEW ZEALAND'S 1988 MAXI-YACHT

The acknowledged aim of New Zealand's 1988 America's Cup challenge was to recreate the excitement and spirit of those years under New York State's Supreme Court–endorsed Deed of Gift for the event, though without trying to return to the long past J-boat days. Syndicate chief Michael Fay, in his official press release, said it was not his attempt to copy or mimic the J's era or any other period in the long history of the world's most enduring international sporting event. "We have taken an initiative both to challenge in 1988 and to do so in a completely different class of boat that will restore some of the old-time grandeur to the event," promised Fay.

The Mercury Bay Boating Club challenge, lodged in the name of Michael Fay, mirrored the terms of the Deed of Gift. And it does so right down to the required essential technical details about the hull and rig.

SAN DIEGO YACHT CLUB AND DENNIS CONNER

For the 1988 contest, two catamarans were designed by John K. Marshall. The hulls were built by RD Boatworks in Capistrano Beach, California, and the sails by Scaled Composites, Inc., in Mojave, California. The first one had a conventional soft sail, code number S1, and the second cat had a winged rig. It was this last one, US-1, that raced for the 1988 America's Cup under skipper Dennis Conner.

The races were planned for September 7 to 9 off San Diego, California; winner of two of the three matches took home the Cup. *Stars & Stripes* raced against the huge ninety-foot mono-hull challenger *New Zealand KZ-1*. Alternate courses were laid out: the first race on September 7, 1988, was forty nautical miles long with one windward leg (twenty miles) and the return with a wind speed of seven to nine knots. *Stars & Stripes* beat *New Zealand* by eighteen minutes, fifteen seconds. The second race, on September 9, consisted of a triangular course of thirty-nine nautical miles (thirteen miles by leg, first windward, two and three reaching leg) with a wind speed of six to fifteen knots. Conner maneuvered his sixty-foot wing-sail catamaran to the second of two consecutive wins; *Stars & Stripes* beat *New Zealand* by twenty-one minutes, ten seconds.

As wrote Tom Coat, the 1988 America's Cup was "a Cup of controversy," but it was also, in the spirit of the tradition of this event, a fantastic technical challenge on both sides.

FROM 1992 AND BEYOND

The International America's Cup Class

Dimension	IACC	12-Metre
LOA	75 ft.	65 ft.
LWL	57 ft.	45 ft.
Beam	18 ft.	12 ft.
Draft	13 ft.	9 ft.
Mast Height	110 ft.	86 ft.
Main and Jib	3,000 sq. ft	2,000 sq. ft
Spinnaker	4,500 sq. ft	2,500 sq. ft
Displacement	37,000 lbs	56,000 lbs

The 1992 America's Cup race series featured several firsts for the historic regatta. Among those firsts, twelve challengers, the largest number of countries ever, filed challengers, with each posting a $150,000 performance bond in September 1990.

The new seventy-five-foot, high-tech International America's Cup Class (IACC) yacht is a class of sailing vessel developed especially for the America's Cup competition. These yachts, while not identical, are all designed to a particular formula so as to make the boats involved in a competition roughly comparable while still giving individuals the freedom to experiment with the details of their designs. The class was established prior to the 1992 America's Cup because of perceived shortcomings of the 12-metre class, which had been used in the America's Cup matches since 1958.

The governing factor of designing an IACC yacht is a mathematical formula that challenges designers to find the best combination of speed-producing factors. The formula considers sail area, length and displacement. It is the job of America's Cup designers to use this rule to design boats that have never been raced in an America's Cup challenge and produce the best boat for the wind and sea conditions of the part of the world the match may be held. The rule encourages tradeoffs in design areas, with the realization that greater strength in one area must be paid for with weakness in another. The designer's challenge is finding the right combination.

The crew of an IACC yacht consists of seventeen: bowman, foredeck, halyards/pitman, spinnaker trimmer, six grinders, starboard headsail trimmer, port headsail trimmer, mainsheet trimmer, helmsman, tactician, navigator and the owner or his representative.

A totally new rule was established after 1988. This has produced three fine matches in 1992, 1995 and 2000. Equally fine racing was achieved in Auckland in 2003. Boats of the IACC class are larger than 12-metre yachts with much finer and lighter hulls utilizing composite construction. The ballast-to-displacement ratio of these boats is remarkably high, with a deep lead bulb of about forty-four thousand pounds supported by a slim steel strut.

New classes require several cycles for an optimum boat type to emerge. In the case of the IACC, the process was rapid principally because of the brilliant and aggressive research and development program devised by American Bill Koch for his *America³* syndicate. Building four boats (by Custom Sailboats of Bristol, Rhode Island) with much experimentation led Koch to the optimum proportions, including a progressive narrowing of beam, a trend followed by his successors. Bill Koch and his relief helmsman, Buddy Melges, won the 1992 America's Cup match in decisive style against Italy.

Chapter 11
Sailing Lingo and Mariners' Manners

ABAFT: toward the stern of a boat

ARDENT: used to describe the tendency of a boat to turn into the wind

BACK: a counterclockwise wind shift

BALLOON JIB: a very full cut jib sail used for reaching

BEAM: the width of a boat

BEAR OFF: turning away from the wind

BEAT / BEATING: sailing into the wind; sailing upwind, usually by tacking

BOW: the forward part of a hull

BOWSPRIT: a spar projecting horizontally from the bow

CATAMARAN: a boat with two connected hulls placed side by side

CATBOAT: a boat with one mast and one sail

CENTERBOARD: a plate set on the center line of a boat that can be raised or lowered

CLIPPER BOW: a nearly vertical bow that is concave in profile

CLOSE HAULED: sailing as close to the wind as possible with sails hardened right in

CLUB BOOM: a boom for a jib, staysail or gaff topsail

COVERING: staying between the competition and the next mark

CROSS CUT SAILS: sail made of cloth that runs at right angles to the leach

DEADWOOD: timbers between the hull and the keel

DISPLACEMENT: a boat's weight

DRAFT: a boat's depth below the water

DROP KEEL: same as centerboard

FIN KEEL: a keel built externally of the hull with a ballast keel attached

FOOT: to ease the sails on a beat, bearing off to pick up speed

FOREDECK: area between the mast and the forestay; spinnaker pole is stored here

FORESAIL: the sail attached to the aft side of the foremast

FRIGATE: a class of sailing warship roughly the size of a modern cruiser

GALLEY: a food preparation space

GRINDERS: rotating handles used to turn the winches

GUN PORT: an opening in the side of a ship through which a gun can be fired

HALYARD: the rope or wire by which a sail is hoisted

HEADER: a shift in wind direction toward the bow

HEAD UP: turning toward the wind

HULL: the body of the boat—usually 1.5 to 2 inches thick

JIBE/JIBING: the act of turning away from the wind so that it crosses the stern

KEEL: an attachment on the bottom of the hull or a boat's longitudinal backbone

KNOT: a measure of speed, roughly equal to one nautical mile per hour

LAYLINE: an imaginary line by which a boat can make the mark without tacking

LEEWARD: away from the wind

LEG O' MUTTON: a Marconi or jib head sail

LIFT: a shift in wind direction toward the stern

LOA: length over all

LUFFING: a maneuver in which the leeward boat turns up into the wind, forcing his opponent to windward, causing that boat's sails to "luff," or flap

LUGGER: a small coasting vessel

LWL: length on the waterline

MAIN: this sail remains up at all times; other sails are changed frequently

MAINSAIL: the sail attached to the mainmast

MARTINGALE: a vertical spar (spreader) under the bowsprit as a support aid

NOBLE: see "ardent"; same as "proud"

OVERHANG: either the forward or aft end of a hull that is not in water

PACKET: a sailing vessel making regular commercial or passenger voyages

PINCHING: sailing too close to the wind

PORT TACK: when the wind is coming over the port (left) side

PROUD: see "ardent"; same as "noble"

RATING RULE: a formula that attempts to determine a boat's potential speed

REACHING: a boat is close reaching when the wind is forward of the beam; beam reaching when the wind is abeam; and broad reaching when the wind is abaft the beam

REEFING: bunching a portion of sail on the boom

RUNNING: sailing before the wind with sheets eased

SANDBAGGER: a sailboat on which bags of sand were used to increase tacking stability

SCHOONER: a boat of two or more masts, fore and aft rigged

SHEATHING: usually thin copper sheets attached to the underwater hull

SLACK: to ease out a line

SLOOP: a single-masted boat with one sail aft of the mast and jib(s) forward

SPINNAKER: a large balloon-shaped sail used before the wind

SPOON BOW: an overhanging convex bow

STARBOARD TACK: sailing with the wind coming across the starboard (right) side of the boat

TACKING: changing direction by heading into the wind and onto the opposite tack

TIME ALLOWANCE: the amount of time a boat must allow another

TONNAGE: a method used to determine the size of a boat for customs purposes

TOPMAST: an additional spar attached to the top of a mast

TRANSOM: the flat back of the boat

TRAVELER: a line that moves on a track to control the angle of the mainsail

TRIM: to adjust or pull in a sail

TRUCK: the top of the mast; the bottom is the heel

TRUNNEL: wooden dowels used to fasten two pieces of wood

VEER: a clockwise wind shift

WINCH: a mechanical device used to assist in pulling in the sails

WINDWARD MARK: the mark that ends a beat

YACHT: a large boat or ship used for pleasure

Mariners' Manners Matter in Match Racing

A yacht tacking to starboard has the right of way over a port-tack yacht. When both boats are on the same tack, the windward boat must stay clear of the leeward boat.

At a mark, the boat that has an inside overlap has the right of way while rounding—only if the overlap was established two boat lengths before the mark. The outside boat must stay clear.

A boat that is over the starting line early must clear itself by going back across the line after the start and restart.

Umpires will hail the boats for any rule infringements. The offending boat must then do a penalty 270-degree turn (or more) to clear itself before continuing to the next mark.

Chapter 12
A Gallery of Challengers, Defenders and Contenders

This October 8, 1934 photo shows Chandler M. Hovey at the helm of the Boston-built *Yankee*. The *Yankee* sought the right to defend the Cup against Sopwith's *Endeavour*. *Associated Press.*

Former U.S. Navy Secretary Charles Francis Adams (in soft hat) sailing aboard the *Yankee* from Newport to New London to join the New York Yacht Club cruise. *Associated Press, 1934.*

The American 12-metre defender, the *Columbia*, finished the September 25, 1958 race a full mile ahead of the *Sceptre*. *Spectator's snapshot.*

The 1958 12-metre British challenger the *Sceptre* raced against the American defender, the *Columbia*, in Rhode Island Sound. *Period postcard.*

The *Endeavour II* in Marblehead, Massachusetts, for a regatta, circa 1938. *Period postcard.*

The 12-metre yacht *Liberty* (right), with Dennis Conner at the helm, beats the yacht *Defender* to the start of the second race in the America's Cup trials off Newport, July 28, 1983. *Associated Press.*

Australia II sails to a win over the Italian yacht *Azzurra* in the challenger trials in Rhode Island Sound, August 2, 1983. *Associated Press.*

The 1988 challenger, *New Zealand*, with a waterline length of approximately ninety feet, was the largest racing sloop constructed since the J-boats. *Official New Zealand syndicate photo.*

Appendix

Historical Chronology

1851
The *America* wins against the British squadron; there is no second place.

1870
Cambria, the British challenger, loses against fourteen New York Yacht Club yachts in New York Harbor. The *Magic* is winner of record.

1871
New York Yacht Club used two yachts, *Columbia* and *Sappho* (allowed for the last time), and defeated the English boat *Livonia*.

1876
Madeleine defeats the *Countess of Dufferin*.

1881
Atalanta from Canada loses 2–0 to *Mischief*.

1885
Centerboard cutter *Puritan* wins over England's *Genesta* 2–0.

1886
The *Mayflower*, another Burgess design for the New York Yacht Club, bests England's *Galatea* 2–0.

1887

A "hat trick" for Burgess; his third win, *Volunteer*, over Scotland's *Thistle*, 2–0.

1893

A truly great design, Nat Herreshoff creates *Vigilant* and wins 3–0 against *Valkyrie*.

1895

Herreshoff's *Defender* defeats the *Valkyrie II*.

1899

Sir Thomas Lipton's *Shamrock* loses to *Columbia* 3–0.

1901

Herreshoff's *Columbia* wins again 3–0 over *Shamrock II*.

1903

Sixteen thousand square feet of sail on the Herreshoff-designed *Reliance* triumphs over Lipton's *Shamrock III*.

1920

The First World War and other events leave a gap in challenges until Lipton, on *Shamrock IV*, races against Herreshoff's last Cup boat, *Resolute*, losing 3–2.

1930

The boats of the J-class series debut with masts as tall as 165 feet and over 80 feet length. Vanderbilt's *Enterprise* meets Lipton's *Shamrock V* in Newport, Rhode Island, winning 4–0.

1937

Ranger beats *Endeavour II*.

1958

Columbia over England's *Sceptre*, 4–0.

1962

Australia challenges with Alan Payne's *Gretel*, losing 4–1 to *Weatherly*.

1964

Constellation swamps England's *Sovereign*, 4–0.

1967

Australia's *Dame Pattie* loses to Sparkman and Stephen's *Intrepid*, 4–0.

1970

The introduction of the multiple-challenger concept. *Gretel II* defeats *France I*, and Sweden's *Sveridge* to challenge *Intrepid*.

1974

Dennis Conner as helmsman on *Courageous* beats *Intrepid* to defend. *Courageous* goes on to defeat Alan Bond's Australian boat *Southern Cross*, 4–0.

1977

Ted Turner's *Courageous* whips the *Australia*, 4–0, which had defeated *Gretel II*, *France I* and Sweden's *Sveridge* to become the challenger.

1980

Freedom with Dennis Conner defeats Ted Turner and Russell Long, then a historic win over Bond's *Australia*, 4–1.

1983

The stage was set. The so-called winged keel helped Australia to wrest the Cup from the New York Yacht Club after 132 years as the *Australia II* wins 4–3 over the New York Yacht Club's *Liberty*. The Cup leaves the NYYC and goes to Perth, Australia.

1987

A true world match: thirteen challengers, six from the United States. *Stars & Stripes* from the San Diego Yacht Club with a Conner-Burnham team slamming Australia's defender the *Kookaburra III* in four straight.

1988

A lopsided match between a giant *New Zealand* maxi-boat against Dennis Conner's double-hulled catamaran *Stars & Stripes*. The San Diego Yacht Club's *Stars & Stripes* won 2–0 over the *New Zealand*.

1992

Bill Koch aboard his Bristol, Rhode Island Custom Sailboats–built *America*[3] successfully defended the Cup against Italy's *Il Moro di Venizia*.

1995

Peter Blake and his *Black Magic* outsailed *Young America* in 1995, returning the Cup to New Zealand.

2000

New Zealand with *Black Magic* keeps the Cup by sweeping Italy's *Luna Rossa*.

2003

World-class sailing by Switzerland's *Alinghi* takes the Cup away from *Black Magic*.

2007

Alinghi whips Emirates Team *New Zealand* 5–2.

2010

Golden Gate Yacht Club trimaran *BMW Oracle* takes the Cup 2–0 over Société Nautique de Geneve catamaran *Alinghi*.

Notes

1. In vernacular British English and Irish English, "the Antipodes" is sometimes used to refer to Australia and New Zealand and "Antipodeans" to their inhabitants. Strictly speaking, the antipodes of Britain and Ireland are in the Pacific Ocean, south of New Zealand. The antipodes of Australia are in the North Atlantic Ocean, while parts of Spain and Portugal are antipodal to New Zealand. (Source: Wikipedia.)
2. Simpson, *Herreshoff Yachts*, 61–64.
3. *Century Magazine*, "Cup Defenders Old and New."
4. Ibid.
5. In 1983, Science Applications International Corporation (SAIC) became involved in the America's Cup after the United States lost the prized trophy for the first time in history. The loss of the Cup was symbolic of worldwide challenges to American technological leadership. Immediately after the 1983 races, it was clear that the Australians had an innovative technical design—the winged keel. But more importantly, as was later learned, they had demonstrated a systematic approach to the process of design. That process included a balance between innovation, engineering analysis and rigorous testing that was lacking in the U.S. program. The Australians fundamentally surpassed the United States in technology areas believed to be U.S. strengths.
6. The upward movement of a ship that is moving up and down in heavy seas.
7. Here it is worthy to note that with the exception of the *Mischief*, which was constructed of iron, the preceding defenders had been of wood. The *Priscilla* was also built of iron, but she did not come up to the standard of the *Puritan*, and wood, therefore, continued to have preference.

8. Yachts at first were measured for rating, or classification, by their tonnage. At first, tonnage was obtained by multiplying the length times the beam times the depth. About 1800, it was determined that most vessels averaged a depth equal to one-half the beam. Because of cargo in the hold, depth was often difficult to measure, so the rule was changed to length times beam times one-half the beam. This rule was used for all shipping for the purpose of taxation; it was also used for the rating of yachts. As beam was measured twice and depth not at all, by making a narrow and deep model the tonnage (rating) was much reduced; thus, the narrow English cutter was developed, and as the development went on, yachts having an actual displacement of twice their measured tonnage were finally built. To the extreme, British yachts got to be seven times as long as they were wide before the rule broke down and a change was made.

In America, the principal measurements were based on waterline length until we finally built freakish-looking yachts whose length overall was twice the length on the waterline. Then most of the yacht clubs adopted the New York Yacht Club's Universal Rule, which has satisfactorily controlled hull proportions.

The International Rule used in Europe and England, and a later rule, calls for the same proportion of draft and displacement for waterline length but controls the overhang in a different way. (Source: *The Writings of L. Francis Herreshoff*, Rudder Publishing Co., 1946.)

The International America's Cup Class is a class of sailing vessels that was developed for the America's Cup competition. These yachts, while not identical, are all designed to a particular formula so as to make the boats involved in a competition roughly comparable while still giving individuals the freedom to experiment with the details of their designs. The class was established prior to the 1992 America's Cup because of perceived shortcomings of the 12-metre class, which had been used in the America's Cup since 1958. Previously, J-class yachts were used.

The International Rule for measurement has changed several times until now, in the first decade of the twenty-first century, the International America's Cup Class rule controls the yachts' rating. Sail numbers are issued according to the date the ACM Measurement Committee decides the hull has reached a certain stage of completion. The number comes in two parts: the country of ownership represented by the three-letter prefix, and the hull number. The country code changes as the hull is transferred from country to country. (Source: Wikipedia.)

9. Copen, "Race for the America's Cup."

10. T.O.M. Sopwith noted aircraft manufacturer of WWI Royal Air Force fighter the Sopwith Camel.
11. The reader is reminded that this quoted news report was originally written when the *Columbia* and the *Constitution* were still in trials and the defender had not yet been selected.
12. So called because of its width, which allowed almost infinite adjustment of the camber of the foot of the mainsail.
13. Simpson, *Herreshoff Yachts*.

Bibliography

American Monthly Review (August 1899).

Baker, Ray Stannard. "The Racing Yacht: Its Points and Its Paces." *McClure's Magazine* (October 1899).

Bavier, Robert N., Jr. *America's Cup Fever*. New York: Ziff-Davis Publishing, 1980.

Century Magazine 46, no. 4. "Cup Defenders Old and New," August 1893.

Copen, Oliver Bronson. "The Race for the America's Cup." *Country Life in America* 4, no. 4 (August 1903).

Financial Times, July 27, 1920.

Frank Leslie's Popular Monthly (September 1899).

Hammond, Geoffrey F. *Showdown in Newport*. New York: Walden Publications, 1974.

Hemment, John C. "The New York Yacht Club." *Munsey's Magazine* (July 1899).

Herreshoff, L. Francis. *An Introduction to Yachting*. New York: Sheridan House, 1963.

Hoyt, Edwin P. *The Defenders*. Cranberry, NJ: A.S. Barnes and Co., Inc., 1969.

Monsey's Magazine (September 1895).

New York Times, April 25, 1914.

Popular Mechanics, 1914.

Scientific American, August 12, 1899; October 14, 1899; May 11, 1901; May 25, 1901; April 11, 1903; April 25, 1903; May 9, 1903; June 27, 1903.

Simpson, Richard V. *The America's Cup Yachts*. Charleston, SC: Arcadia Publishing, 1999.

About the Author

R ichard V. Simpson is a native Rhode Islander who has always lived within walking distance to Narragansett Bay; first in the Edgewood section of Cranston and in Bristol, where he has lived since 1960.

A graphic designer by trade, he has worked in advertising, printing, display and textile design studios. After retiring in 1996 from a twenty-nine-year Federal Civil Service career with the U.S. Navy in Newport, he began a second career as an author of books on subjects of historical interest in Rhode Island's East Bay, with his principal focus on Bristol.

This is Richard's sixteenth published title and the third with America's Cup yachts as its subject. He continues as a contributing editor for the national monthly *Antiques & Collecting Magazine*, in which eighty-five of his articles have appeared, a position he has enjoyed since 1985.

Bristol's famous Independence Day celebration and parade has also been the subject of Richard's pen. His 1989 *Independence Day* is the singular authoritative book on the subject, and his many anecdotal Fourth of July articles have appeared in the local *Bristol Phoenix* and the *Providence Journal*.

Other Books by Richard V. Simpson
A History of the Italian-Roman Catholic Church in Bristol, RI (1967)
Independence Day: How the Day Is Celebrated in Bristol, RI (1989)
Old St. Mary's: Mother Church in Bristol, RI (1994)
Bristol, Rhode Island: In the Mount Hope Lands of King Philip (1996)
Bristol, Rhode Island: The Bristol Renaissance (1998)
America's Cup Yachts: The Rhode Island Connection (1999)
Building the Mosquito Fleet: U.S. Navy's First Torpedo Boats (2001)
Bristol: Montaup to Poppasquash (2002)
Bristol, Rhode Island: A Postcard History (2005)
Narragansett Bay: A Postcard History (2005)
Herreshoff Yachts: Seven Generations of Industrialists, Inventors and Ingenuity in Bristol (2007)
Historic Bristol: Tales From an Old Rhode Island Seaport (2008)

Books by Richard V. Simpson and Nancy J. Devin
Portsmouth, Rhode Island: Ancestral Lands of the Narragansett (1997)
Tiverton and Little Compton, RI: Wampanoag Country (1997)
Tiverton and Little Compton, Rhode Island: Volume II (1998)